Modern Critical Interpretations

Joseph Conrad's
Nostromo

Modern Critical Interpretations

The Oresteia
Beowulf
The General Prologue to
    The Canterbury Tales
The Pardoner's Tale
The Knight's Tale
The Divine Comedy
Exodus
Genesis
The Gospels
The Iliad
The Book of Job
Volpone
Doctor Faustus
The Revelation of St.
    John the Divine
The Song of Songs
Oedipus Rex
The Aeneid
The Duchess of Malfi
Antony and Cleopatra
As You Like It
Coriolanus
Hamlet
Henry IV, Part I
Henry IV, Part II
Henry V
Julius Caesar
King Lear
Macbeth
Measure for Measure
The Merchant of Venice
A Midsummer Night's
    Dream
Much Ado About
    Nothing
Othello
Richard II
Richard III
The Sonnets
Taming of the Shrew
The Tempest
Twelfth Night
The Winter's Tale
Emma
Mansfield Park
Pride and Prejudice
The Life of Samuel
    Johnson
Moll Flanders
Robinson Crusoe
Tom Jones
The Beggar's Opera
Gray's Elegy
Paradise Lost
The Rape of the Lock
Tristram Shandy
Gulliver's Travels

Evelina
The Marriage of Heaven
    and Hell
Songs of Innocence and
    Experience
Jane Eyre
Wuthering Heights
Don Juan
The Rime of the Ancient
    Mariner
Bleak House
David Copperfield
Hard Times
A Tale of Two Cities
Middlemarch
The Mill on the Floss
Jude the Obscure
The Mayor of
    Casterbridge
The Return of the Native
Tess of the D'Urbervilles
The Ode of Keats
Frankenstein
Vanity Fair
Barchester Towers
The Prelude
The Red Badge of
    Courage
The Scarlet Letter
The Ambassadors
Daisy Miller, The Turn
    of the Screw, and
    Other Tales
The Portrait of a Lady
Billy Budd, Benito Cer-
    eno, Bartleby the Scriv-
    ener, and Other Tales
Moby-Dick
The Tales of Poe
Walden
Adventures of
    Huckleberry Finn
The Life of Frederick
    Douglass
Heart of Darkness
Lord Jim
Nostromo
A Passage to India
Dubliners
A Portrait of the Artist as
    a Young Man
Ulysses
Kim
The Rainbow
Sons and Lovers
Women in Love
1984
Major Barbara

Man and Superman
Pygmalion
St. Joan
The Playboy of the
    Western World
The Importance of Being
    Earnest
Mrs. Dalloway
To the Lighthouse
My Antonia
An American Tragedy
Murder in the Cathedral
The Waste Land
Absalom, Absalom!
Light in August
Sanctuary
The Sound and the Fury
The Great Gatsby
A Farewell to Arms
The Sun Also Rises
Arrowsmith
Lolita
The Iceman Cometh
Long Day's Journey Into
    Night
The Grapes of Wrath
Miss Lonelyhearts
The Glass Menagerie
A Streetcar Named
    Desire
Their Eyes Were
    Watching God
Native Son
Waiting for Godot
Herzog
All My Sons
Death of a Salesman
Gravity's Rainbow
All the King's Men
The Left Hand of
    Darkness
The Brothers Karamazov
Crime and Punishment
Madame Bovary
The Interpretation of
    Dreams
The Castle
The Metamorphosis
The Trial
Man's Fate
The Magic Mountain
Montaigne's Essays
Remembrance of Things
    Past
The Red and the Black
Anna Karenina
War and Peace

These and other titles in preparation

Modern Critical Interpretations

Joseph Conrad's
Nostromo

Edited and with an introduction by

Harold Bloom
Sterling Professor of the Humanities
Yale University

Chelsea House Publishers ◊ *1987*

NEW YORK ◊ NEW HAVEN ◊ PHILADELPHIA

©1987 by Chelsea House Publishers, a division of Chelsea
House Educational Communications, Inc.
    133 Christopher Street, New York, NY 10014
    345 Whitney Avenue, New Haven, CT 06511
    5014 West Chester Pike, Edgemont, PA 19028

Introduction © 1986 by Harold Bloom

Printed and bound in the United States of America

∞ The paper used in this publication meets the minimum
requirements of the American National Standard for
Permanence of Paper for Printed Library Materials,
Z39.48-1984.

Library of Congress Cataloging-in-Publication Data
Joseph Conrad's Nostromo.

    (Modern critical interpretations)
    Bibliography: p.
    Includes index.
    Summary: A collection of eight critical essays on
Conrad's novel, arranged in chronological order of
publication.
    1. Conrad, Joseph, 1857–1924. Nostromo. [1. Conrad,
Joseph, 1857–1924. Nostromo. 2. English literature —
History and criticism]   I. Bloom, Harold.   II. Series.
PR6005.04N5936 1987   823'.912   86–20695
ISBN 1–55546–017–8 (alk. paper)

Contents

Editor's Note / vii

Introduction / 1
HAROLD BLOOM

"The Great Mirage": Conrad and *Nostromo* / 7
ROBERT PENN WARREN

Guardianship of the Treasure: *Nostromo* / 23
DOROTHY VAN GHENT

Continuities and Discontinuities: *Middlemarch* and *Nostromo* / 39
GEORGE LEVINE

Revelation and Repression in Conrad's *Nostromo* / 43
KIERNAN RYAN

Nostromo: Conrad's Organicist Philosophy of History / 57
T. MCALINDON

The Limits of Irony / 69
MARTIN PRICE

Four Views of the Hero / 81
STEPHEN K. LAND

Silver and Silence: Dependent Currencies in *Nostromo* / 103
AARON FOGEL

Chronology / 127

Contributors / 129

Bibliography / 131

Acknowledgments / 135

Index / 137

Editor's Note

This book brings together what I judge to be the best criticism available upon the novel that is Joseph Conrad's masterwork, *Nostromo*. The essays are reprinted here in the chronological order of their original publication. I am grateful to David Parker for his erudition and judgment in helping to edit this volume.

My introduction addresses itself to the enigma—rhetorical and psychological—of just how Conrad persuades us of Nostromo's magnificence, his sublime presence and charismatic authority. Robert Penn Warren, whose novels and poetry alike show the influence of Conrad, begins the chronological sequence with his classic appreciation of *Nostromo*'s moral and dramatic strength as a narrative.

Dorothy Van Ghent explores the many aspects of "treasure" in *Nostromo*, a word which resonates throughout the novel on every level from literal to folklore to myth. In a brief introduction from his larger comparison of *Nostromo* and *Middlemarch*, George Levine sees that the distance between the two seemingly disparate novels is "by no means absolute." A sense of the contradictory impulses warring with one another, as they always do in Conrad, is conveyed by Kiernan Ryan, whose key terms of "revelation" and "repression" deeply contaminate one another, which is again inevitable where the text of Conrad is concerned.

Can a nihilist (assuming Conrad is that) have a philosophy of history? T. McAlindon relates Carlyle's organicist vision of history to Conrad's in *Nostromo*, asserting that Conrad both emanates from Carlyle and also exposes the limitations of Carlyle's strenuously faithless faith. Martin Price calls into question any judgments made by moral readings of Conrad in his subtle demonstration of how Conrad drives apart the heroic and the authentic without abandoning a desire for both. Stephen K. Land, also exploring Conradian paradox, confronts us with the puzzle that while only *Nostromo* among Conrad's novels has four central figures (Nostromo himself, Decoud,

Charles Gould, Monygham) rather than one, Conrad does not allow himself to work through the narratives of all of them.

In what seems to me the best analysis *Nostromo* has yet received, Aaron Fogel reads the novel as an instance of forced dialogue between agonists, Oedipal strivers against themselves as well as against one another. Fogel, in the tonalities of contemporary advanced literary criticism, returns us to the difficulty that enchants and perplexes every critic of *Nostromo*: how could Conrad achieve a fresh representation of the natural sublime, the greatness of the natural man, in his hero, while affirming also the silent abyss of the skeptics and nihilists?

Introduction

In Conrad's "Youth" (1898), Marlow gives us a brilliant description of the sinking of the *Judea*:

> "Between the darkness of earth and heaven she was burning fiercely upon a disc of purple sea shot by the blood-red play of gleams; upon a disc of water glittering and sinister. A high, clear flame, an immense and lonely flame, ascended from the ocean, and from its summit the black smoke poured continuously at the sky. She burned furiously; mournful and imposing like a funeral pile kindled in the night, surrounded by the sea, watched over by the stars. A magnificent death had come like a grace, like a gift, like a reward to that old ship at the end of her laborious day. The surrender of her weary ghost to the keeper of the stars and sea was stirring like the sight of a glorious triumph. The masts fell just before daybreak, and for a moment there was a burst and turmoil of sparks that seemed to fill with flying fire the night patient and watchful, the vast night lying silent upon the sea. At daylight she was only a charred shell, floating still under a cloud of smoke and bearing a glowing mass of coal within.
>
> "Then the oars were got out, and the boats forming in a line moved round her remains as if in procession—the longboat leading. As we pulled across her stern a slim dart of fire shot out viciously at us, and suddenly she went down, head first, in a great hiss of steam. The unconsumed stern was the last to sink; but the paint had gone, had cracked, had peeled off, and there were no letters, there was no word, no stubborn device that was like her soul, to flash at the rising sun her creed and her name."

The apocalyptic vividness is enhanced by the visual namelessness of the "unconsumed stern," as though the creed of Christ's people maintained both its traditional refusal to violate the Second Commandment, and its traditional affirmation of its not-to-be-named God. With the *Judea*, Conrad sinks the romance of youth's illusions, but like all losses in Conrad this submersion in the destructive element is curiously dialectical, since only experiential loss allows for the compensation of an imaginative gain in the representation of artistic truth. Originally the ephebe of Flaubert and of Flaubert's "son," Maupassant, Conrad was reborn as the narrative disciple of Henry James, the James of *The Spoils of Poynton* and *What Maisie Knew* rather than the James of the final phase.

Ian Watt convincingly traces the genesis of Marlow to the way that "James developed the indirect narrative approach through the sensitive central intelligence of one of the characters." Marlow, whom James derided as "that preposterous magic mariner," actually represents Conrad's swerve away from the excessive strength of James's influence upon him. By always "mixing himself up with the narrative," in James's words, Marlow guarantees an enigmatic reserve that increases the distance between the impressionistic techniques of Conrad and James. Though there is little valid comparison that can be made between Conrad's greatest achievements and the hesitant, barely fictional status of Pater's *Marius the Epicurean*, Conrad's impressionism is as extreme and solipsistic as Pater's. There is a definite parallel between the fates of Sebastian Van Storck (in Pater's *Imaginary Portraits*) and Decoud in *Nostromo*.

In his 1897 Preface to *The Nigger of the "Narcissus,"* Conrad famously insisted that his creative task was "before all to make you *see*." He presumably was aware that he thus joined himself to a line of prose seers whose latest representatives were Carlyle, Ruskin, and Pater. There is a movement in that group from Carlyle's exuberant "Natural Supernaturalism" through Ruskin's paganization of Evangelical fervor to Pater's evasive and skeptical Epicurean materialism, with its eloquent suggestion that all we can see is the flux of sensations. Conrad exceeds Pater in the reduction of impressionism to a state of consciousness where the seeing narrator is hopelessly mixed up with the seen narrative. James may seem an impressionist when compared to Flaubert, but alongside of Conrad he is clearly shown to be a kind of Platonist, imposing forms and resolutions upon the flux of human relations by an exquisite formal geometry altogether his own.

To observe that Conrad is metaphysically less of an Idealist is hardly to argue that he is necessarily a stronger novelist than his master, James. It may suggest though that Conrad's originality is more disturbing than that of

James, and may help explain why Conrad, rather than James, became the dominant influence upon the generation of American novelists that included Hemingway, Fitzgerald, and Faulkner. The cosmos of *The Sun Also Rises*, *The Great Gatsby*, and *As I Lay Dying* derives from *Heart of Darkness* and *Nostromo* rather than from *The Ambassadors* and *The Golden Bowl*. Darl Bundren is the extreme inheritor of Conrad's quest to carry impressionism into its heart of darkness in the human awareness that we are only a flux of sensations gazing outwards upon a flux of impressions.

II

An admirer of Conrad is happiest with his five great novels: *Lord Jim* (1900), *Nostromo* (1904), *The Secret Agent* (1907), *Under Western Eyes* (1911), and *Victory* (1914). Subtle and tormented narratives, they form an extraordinarily varied achievement, and despite their common features they can make a reader wonder that they all should have been composed by the same artist. Endlessly enigmatic as a personality and as a formidable moral character, Conrad pervades his own books, a presence not to be put by, an elusive storyteller who yet seems to write a continuous spiritual autobiography. By the general consent of advanced critics and of common readers, Conrad's masterwork is *Nostromo*, where his perspectives are largest, and where his essential originality in the representation of human blindnesses and consequent human affections is at its strongest. Like all overwhelming originalities, Conrad's ensues in an authentic difficulty, which can be assimilated only very slowly, if at all. Repeated rereadings gradually convince me that *Nostromo* is anything but a Conradian litany to the virtue he liked to call "fidelity." The book is tragedy, of a post-Nietzschean sort, despite Conrad's strong contempt for Nietzsche. Decoud, void of all illusions, is self-destroyed because he cannot sustain solitude. Nostromo, perhaps the only persuasive instance of the natural sublime in a twentieth-century hero of fiction, dies "betrayed he hardly knows by what or by whom," as Conrad says. But this is Conrad at his most knowing, and the novel shows us precisely how Nostromo is betrayed, by himself, and by what in himself.

It is a mystery of an overwhelming fiction why it can sustain virtually endless rereadings. *Nostromo*, to me, rewards frequent rereadings in something of the way that *Othello* does; there is always surprise waiting for me. Brilliant as every aspect of the novel is, Nostromo himself is the imaginative center of the book, and yet Nostromo is unique among Conrad's personae, and not a Conradian man whom we could have expected. His creator's description of this central figure as "the Magnificent Capataz, the Man of the People," breathes a writer's love for his most surprising act of the imagination. So does a crucial paragraph from the same source, the Author's Note that Conrad added as a preface thirteen years after the initial publication:

> In his firm grip on the earth he inherits, in his improvidence and generosity, in his lavishness with his gifts, in his manly vanity, in the obscure sense of his greatness and in his faithful devotion with something despairing as well as desperate in its impulses, he is a Man of the People, their very own unenvious force, disdaining to lead but ruling from within. Years afterwards, grown older as the famous Captain Fidanza, with a stake in the country, going about his many affairs followed by respectful glances in the modernized streets of Sulaco, calling on the widow of the cargador, attending the Lodge, listening in unmoved silence to anarchist speeches at the meeting, the enigmatical patron of the new revolutionary agitation, the trusted, the wealthy comrade Fidanza with the knowledge of his moral ruin locked up in his breast, he remains essentially a man of the People. In his mingled love and scorn of life and in the bewildered conviction of having been betrayed, of dying betrayed he hardly knows by what or by whom, he is still of the People, their undoubted Great Man— with a private history of his own.

Despite this "moral ruin," and not because of it, Conrad and his readers share the conviction of Nostromo's greatness, share in his sublime self-recognition. How many persuasive images of greatness, of a natural sublimity, exist in modern fiction? Conrad's may be the last enhanced vision of Natural Man, of the Man of the People, in which anyone has found it possible to believe. Yet Conrad himself characteristically qualifies his own belief in Nostromo, and critics too easily seduced by ironies have weakly misread the merely apparent irony of Conrad's repeated references to Nostromo as "the magnificent Capataz de Cargadores." Magnificent, beyond the reach of all irony, Nostromo manifestly is. It is the magnificence of the natural leader who disdains leadership, yet who loves reputation. Though he is of the People, Nostromo serves no ideal, unlike old Viola the Garibaldino. With the natural genius for command, the charismatic endowment that could make him another Garibaldi, Nostromo nevertheless scorns any such role, in the name of any cause whatsoever. He is a pure Homeric throwback, not wholly unlike Tolstoy's Hadji Murad, except that he acknowledges neither enemies nor friends except for his displaced father, Viola. And he enchants us even as he enchants the populace of Sulaco, though most of all he enchants the skeptical and enigmatic Conrad, who barely defends himself against the enchantment with some merely rhetorical ironies.

Ethos is the daimon, character is fate, in Conrad as in Heracleitus, and Nostromo's tragic fate is the inevitable fulfillment of his desperate grandeur, which Conrad cannot dismiss as mere vanity, despite all his own skepticism. Only Nostromo saves the novel, and Conrad, from nihilism, the nihilism of Decoud's waste in suicide. Nostromo is betrayed partly by Decoud's act of self-destruction, with its use of four ingots of silver to send his body down, but largely by his own refusal to maintain the careless preference for glory over gain which is more than a gesture or a style, which indeed is the authentic mode of being that marks the hero. Nostromo is only himself when he can say, with perfect truth: "My name is known from one end of Sulaco to the other. What more can you do for me?"

III

Towards the end of chapter 10 of part 3, "The Lighthouse," Conrad renders his own supposed verdict upon both Decoud and Nostromo, in a single page, in two parallel sentences a paragraph apart:

> A victim of the disillusioned weariness which is the retribution meted out to intellectual audacity, the brilliant Don Martin Decoud, weighted by the bars of San Tomé silver, disappeared without a trace, swallowed up in the immense indifference of things.

> The magnificent Capataz de Cargadores, victim of the disenchanted vanity which is the reward of audacious action, sat in the weary pose of a hunted outcast through a night of sleeplessness as tormenting as any known to Decoud, his companion in the most desperate affair of his life. And he wondered how Decoud had died.

Decoud's last thought, after shooting himself was: "I wonder how that Capataz died." Conrad seems to leave little to choose between being "a victim of the disillusioned weariness which is the retribution meted out to intellectual audacity" or a "victim of the disenchanted vanity which is the reward of audacious action." The brilliant intellectual and the magnificent man of action are victimized alike for their audacity, and it is a fine irony that "retribution" and "reward" become assimilated to one another. Yet the book is Nostromo's and not Decoud's, and a "disenchanted vanity" is a higher fate than a "disillusioned weariness," if only because an initial enchantment is a nobler state than an initial illusion. True that Nostromo's enchantment was only of and with himself, but that is proper for an Achilles or a Hadji Murad. Decoud dies because he cannot bear solitude, and so cannot bear himself. Nostromo finds death-in-life and then death because he has lost the truth of his vanity, its enchanted insouciance, the *sprezzatura* which he, a plebian, nevertheless had made his authentic self.

Nostromo's triumph, though he cannot know it, is that an image of this authenticity survives him, an image so powerful as to persuade both Conrad and the perceptive reader that even the self-betrayed hero retains an aesthetic dignity that renders his death tragic rather than sordid. Poor Decoud, for all his brilliance, dies a nihilistic death, disappearing "without a trace, swallowed up in the immense indifference of things." Nostromo, after his death, receives an aesthetic tribute beyond all irony, in the superb closing paragraph of the novel:

> Dr. Monygham, pulling round in the police-galley, heard the name pass over his head. It was another of Nostromo's triumphs, the greatest, the most enviable, the most sinister of all. In that true cry of undying passion that seemed to ring aloud from Punta Mala to Azuera and away to the bright line of the horizon, overhung by a big white cloud shining like a mass of solid silver, the genius of the magnificent Capataz de Cargadores dominated the dark gulf containing his conquests of treasure and love.

"The Great Mirage": Conrad and *Nostromo*

Robert Penn Warren

Conrad, in one sense, had little concern for character independently considered. He is no Dickens or Shakespeare, with relish for the mere variety and richness of personality. Rather, for him a character lives in terms of its typical involvement with situation and theme: the fable, the fable as symbol for exfoliating theme, is his central fact. . . .

Conrad writes in *A Personal Record*: "Those who read me know my conviction that the world, the temporal world, rests on a few very simple ideas, so simple that they must be as old as the hills. It rests notably, among others, on the idea of Fidelity." Or again in his tribute to the Merchant Service in 1918, an essay called "Well Done": "For the great mass of mankind the only saving grace that is needed is steady fidelity to what is nearest to hand and heart in the short moment of each human effort." Fidelity and the sense of the job, the discipline of occupation which becomes a moral discipline with its own objective laws, this, for example, is what saves Marlow in *Heart of Darkness* as it had saved the Roman legionaries, those "handy men," when they had ventured into the dark heart of Britain.

Fidelity and the job sense make for the human community, the solidarity in which Conrad finds his final values, "the solidarity of all mankind in simple ideas and sincere emotions." It is through the realization of this community that man cures himself of that "feeling of life-emptiness" which had afflicted the young hero of *The Shadow-Line* before he came to his great test.

The characteristic story for Conrad becomes, then, the relation of

---

man to the human communion. The story may be one of three types: the story of the MacWhirr or the Don Pépé or the Captain Mitchell, the man who lacks imagination and cannot see the "true horror behind the appalling face of things," and who can cling to fidelity and the job; the story of the Kurtz or Decoud, the sinner against human solidarity and the human mission; the story of the redemption, of Lord Jim, Heyst, Dr. Monygham, Flora de Barral, Captain Anthony, Razumov.

The first type of story scarcely engages Conrad. He admires the men of natural virtue, their simplicity, their dogged extroverted sense of obligation and self-respect. But his attitude toward them is ambivalent: they are men "thus fortunate —or thus disdained by destiny or by the sea." They live in a moral limbo of unawareness. They may not be damned like Kurtz or Decoud and achieve that strange, perverse exultation of horror or grim satisfaction by recognizing their own doom, or be saved like Dr. Monygham or Flora de Barral. We may almost say that their significance is in their being, not in their doing, that they have, properly speaking, no "story"; they are the static image of the condition which men who are real and who have real "stories" may achieve by accepting the logic of experience, but which, when earned, has a dynamic value the innocent never know. The man who has been saved may reach the moment of fulfillment when he can spontaneously meet the demands of fidelity, but his spontaneity must have been earned, and only by the fact of its having been earned is it, at last, significant. Therefore, it is the last type of story that engages Conrad most fully, the effort of the alienated, whatever the cause of his alienation, crime or weakness or accident or the "mystic wound," to enter again the human communion. And the crisis of this story comes when the hero recognizes the terms on which he may be saved, the moment, to take Morton Zabel's phrase, of the "terror of the awakening."

In this general connection some critics have been troubled by, or at least have commented on, the fact that Conrad's prefaces and essays, and even his autobiographical writings and letters, seem ambiguous, contradictory, false, or blandly misleading in relation to the fiction. His comments on Fidelity, such as that above from *A Personal Record*, and his remarks on human solidarity seem so far away from the dark inwardness of his work, this inwardness taken either as the story of his heroes or as the nature of his creative process. When we read parts of *A Personal Record*, for example, we see the image of the false Conrad conjured up by reviewers long ago, the image that William McFee complained about: "a two-fisted shipmaster" telling us simply how brave men behave. And we realize how far this image is from the Conrad who suffered from gout, malaria, rheumatism, neuralgia, dyspepsia, insomnia, and nerves; who, after the Congo experience and its moral shock, says of himself, "I lay on my back in dismal lodgings and expected to go out like a burnt-out candle any moment. That was nerves"; who suffered "moments of cruel blankness"; who on one occasion, years later, had two doctors attending him, each unaware of the other, and who at the same time emptied all medicine into the slop; who advised an aspiring writer that "you must search the darkest corners of your heart," and told the successful and simple-souled Galsworthy, a sort of MacWhirr of literature, "the fact is you want more scepticism at the very fountain of your work. Scepticism, the tonic of minds, the tonic of life, the agent of truth—the way of art and salvation"; and who said of his own work, "For me, writing—the only possible writing—is just simply the conversion of nervous force into phrases."

But should we be troubled by this discrepancy between the two Conrads, the Conrad who praised the simple ideas and sincere emotions and the Conrad of the neurotic illnesses and the dark inwardness? No, we should not, but in saying that we should not I mean a little more than what has been offered elsewhere as a resolution of the discrepancy, the notion that the introverted and lonely Conrad, with a sizable baggage of guilts and fears, yearned, even as he mixed some contempt with his yearning, for the simplicity and certainty of the extroverted MacWhirrs of the world. I mean, in addition to this, a corollary of what has been said above about the story of awakening and redemption being the story that engaged Conrad most fully.

Perhaps the corollary can be stated in this fashion: If the central process that engaged Conrad is the process of the earned redemption, that process can only be rendered as "story," and any generalization about it would falsify the process. Instinctively or consciously, Conrad was willing to give the terms of the process, the poles of the situation, as it were, but not an abstract summary. The abstract summary would give no sense of the truth found within, in what, according to the Preface to *The Nigger of the "Narcissus,"* is "that lonely region of stress and strife."

There is another discrepancy, or apparent discrepancy, that we must confront in any serious consideration of Conrad—that between his professions of skepticism and his professions of faith. Already I have quoted his corrosive remark to Galsworthy, but that remark is not as radical as what he says in a letter to R. B. Cunninghame Graham:

> The attitude of cold unconcern is the only reasonable one. Of course, reason is hateful—but why? Because it demonstrates (to those who have courage) that we, living, are out of life—utterly

out of it. The mysteries of a universe made of drops of fire and clods of mud do not concern us in the least. The fate of humanity condemned ultimately to perish from cold is not worth troubling about.

Here, clearly enough, we see the trauma inflicted by nineteenth-century science, a "mystic wound" that Conrad suffered from in company with Hardy, Tennyson, Housman, Stevenson, and most men since their date.

Cold unconcern, an "attitude of perfect indifference" is, as he says in the letter to Galsworthy, "the part of creative power." But this is the same Conrad who speaks of Fidelity and the human communion, and who makes Kurtz cry out in the last horror and Heyst come to his vision of meaning in life. And this is the same Conrad who makes Marlow of *Heart of Darkness* say that what redeems is the "idea only," and makes the devoted Miss Haldin of *Under Western Eyes* say of her dead heroic brother, "Our dear one once told me to remember that men serve always something greater than themselves—the idea."

It is not some, but all, men who must serve the "idea." The lowest and the most vile creature must, in some way, idealize his existence in order to exist, and must find sanctions outside himself. This notion appears over and over in Conrad's fiction. For instance, there is the villainous Ricardo of *Victory*, one of the three almost allegorical manifestations of evil. "As is often the case with lawless natures, Ricardo's faith in any given individual was of a simple, unquestioning character. For a man must have some support in life." Or when Ricardo thinks of the tale of how Heyst had supposedly betrayed Morrison:

> For Ricardo was sincere in his indignation before the elementary principle of loyalty to a chum violated in cold blood, slowly, in a patient duplicity of years. There are standards in villainy as in virtue, and the act as he pictured it to himself acquired an additional horror from the slow pace of that treachery so atrocious and so tame.

Then there is the villain Brown of *Lord Jim*. When, after Jim has allowed him to escape, he falls upon the unsuspecting men of Dain Waris, the act is not a "vulgar massacre":

> Notice that even in this awful outbreak there is a superiority as of a man who carries right—the abstract thing—within the envelope of his common desires. It was not a vulgar and treacherous massacre; it was a lesson, a retribution.

Even bloodthirstiness or villainy must appeal beyond itself to the "idea." The central passage of *Lord Jim*, Stein's speech about the "destructive element," is the basic text for this theme of Conrad:

> A man that is born falls into a dream like a man who falls into the sea. If he tries to climb out into the air as inexperienced people endeavor to do, he drowns—*nicht wahr?* . . . No! I tell you! The way is to the destructive element submit yourself, and with the exertions of your hands and feet in the water make the deep, deep sea keep you up.

I take this, in the context of the action, to read as follows: It is man's fate to be born into the "dream"—the fate of all men. By the dream Conrad here means nothing more or less than man's necessity to justify himself by the "idea," to idealize himself and his actions into moral significance of some order, to find sanctions. But why is the dream like the sea, a "destructive element"? Because man, in one sense, is purely a creature of nature, an animal of black egotism and savage impulses. He should, to follow the metaphor, walk on the dry land of "nature," the real, naturalistic world, and not be dropped into the waters he is so ill equipped to survive in. Those men who take the purely "natural" view, who try to climb out of the sea, who deny the dream and man's necessity to submit to the idea, who refuse to create values that are, quite literally, "super-natural" and therefore human, are destroyed by the dream. They drown in it, and their agony is the agony of their frustrated humanity. Their failure is the failure to understand what is specifically human. They are the Kurtzes, the Browns, in so far as they are villains, but they are also all those isolated ones who are isolated because they have feared to take the full risk of humanity. To conclude the reading of the passage, man, as a natural creature, is not born to swim in the dream, with gills and fins, but if he submits in his own imperfect, "natural" way he can learn to swim and keep himself up, however painfully, in the destructive element. To surrender to the incorrigible and ironical necessity of the "idea," that is man's fate and his only triumph.

Conrad's skepticism is ultimately but a "reasonable" recognition of the fact that man is a natural creature who can rest on no revealed values and can look forward to neither individual immortality nor racial survival. But reason, in this sense, is the denial of life and energy, for against all reason man insists, as man, on creating and trying to live by certain values. These values are, to use Conrad's word, "illusions," but the last wisdom is for man to realize that though his values are illusions, the illusion is necessary, is infinitely precious, is the mark of his human achievement, and is, in the end, his only truth.

From this notion springs the motif of the "true lie," as we may term it, which appears several times in Conrad's fiction. For a first example, we may think of the end of *Heart of Darkness*, when Marlow returns from the Congo to his interview with Kurtz's Intended, whose forehead, in the darkening room, "remained illumined by the unextinguishable light of belief and love." She demands to know her beloved's last words, and Marlow, confronted by her belief and love, manages to say: "The last word he pronounced was— your name." He is not able to tell her the literal truth, the words, "The horror! The horror!" that Kurtz had uttered with his failing breath. If he had done so, "it would have been too dark—too dark altogether . . ." He has, literally, lied, but his lie is a true lie in that it affirms the "idea," the "illusion," belief and love.

Again, in *Under Western Eyes*, Miss Haldin speaks of bringing Razumov, supposedly the friend of her dead brother, to speak to the bereaved mother: "It would be a mercy if mamma could be soothed. You know what she imagines. Some explanation perhaps may be found, or—or even made up, perhaps. It would be no sin."

And even in *Nostromo* the lie that is true, that is no sin, reappears. The incorruptible capataz, dying, is on the verge of telling Mrs. Gould the secret of the stolen treasure, but she will not hear him. When she issues from the room, Dr. Monygham, with the "light of his temperamental enmity to Nostromo" shining in his eyes, demands to know if his long-nourished suspicion of the "incorruptible" Nostromo is correct. He longs to know, to soothe the old wound of his own corruptibility. "He told me nothing," Mrs. Gould says, steadily, and with her charitable lie affirms forever the ideal image of the dead capataz.

Skepticism is the reasonable view of the illusion, but skepticism, the attitude of the intelligence that would be self-sufficient, cannot survive, ironically enough, except by the presence of illusion. The fate of the skeptic Decoud, the "imaginative materialist," who had undertaken to be the natural man in that he had erected passions into duties, is the key parable, among many parables in Conrad, of the meaning of skepticism. Decoud had thought himself outside the human commitments, outside the influence of the "idea," the worshiper of reason, which told him that the only reality is sensation. In so far as his skepticism is "natural," he recognizes the skepticism of Nostromo, the natural man who, "like me, has come casually here to be drawn into the events for which his skepticism as well as mine seems to entertain a sort of passive contempt."

But Decoud's worship of nature and reason is not enough. As soon as he finds himself outside the human orbit, alone with sea and sky, he cannot live. Even skepticism demands belief to feed on; the opposite pole of the essential situation must be present for skepticism to survive.

> Solitude from mere outward condition of existence becomes very swiftly a state of soul in which the affectation of irony and scepticism have no place. . . . After three days of waiting for the sight of some human face, Decoud caught himself entertaining a doubt of his own individuality. It had merged into the world of cloud and water, of natural forces and forms of nature. In our activity alone do we find the sustaining illusion of an independent existence as against the whole scheme of things of which we form a helpless part.

Decoud has reached the ultimate stage of skepticism: his skepticism has dissolved his identity into nature. But even at this moment of his spiritual, and physical, death, he experiences the "first moral sentiment of his manhood," the vague awareness of a "misdirected life." Now both intelligence and passion are "swallowed up easily in this great unbroken solitude of waiting without faith." In this "sadness of a sceptical mind," he beholds "the universe as a succession of incomprehensible images." His act of shooting himself and letting his body fall into the sea is merely the literal repetition of an already accomplished fate: he is "swallowed up in the immense indifference of things."

How are we to reconcile the moral of the story of Decoud, or of Heyst, with Conrad's statements of a radical skepticism—or with even a radical pessimism, the notion of man as a savage animal driven by a black ego? Can we say, as F. R. Leavis says, that "*Nostromo* was written by a Decoud who wasn't a complacent dilettante, but was positively drawn towards those capable of 'investing their activities with spiritual value'— Monygham, Giorgio Viola, Señor Avellanos, Charles Gould"? Or can we say, as Albert Guerard, Jr., says, that against man's heart of darkness we can "throw up only the barrier of semi-military ethics; courage, order, tradition and unquestioned discipline; and as a last resort, the stoic's human awareness of his own plight, a pessimism '*plus sombre que la nuit*'"? Both these statements are, in one sense, true. They do describe the bias of Conrad's temperament as I read it, but they do not describe, to my satisfaction at least, the work that Conrad produced out of that temperament. We must sometimes force ourselves to remember that the act of creation is not simply a projection of temperament, but a criticism and purging of temperament.

If Conrad repudiates the Decouds of the world, even as they speak with, as Leavis says, his "personal *timbre*," he also has for the MacWhirrs of the world, the creatures of "semi-military ethics," a very ambivalent attitude, and some of the scorn of a man who knows at least a little of the cost of awareness and the difficulty of virtue. In other words, his work itself is at center dramatic: it is about the cost of awareness and the difficulty of virtue, and his characteristic story is the story of struggle and, sometimes, of redemption. Skepticism, he wrote to Galsworthy, is "the tonic of minds, the tonic of life, the agent of truth—the way of art and salvation." This is, I suppose, a parallel to Hardy's famous statement: "if way to the Better there be, it exacts a full look at the Worst." It is a way of saying that truth is not easy, but it is also a way of saying that truth, and even salvation, may be possible. Must we choose between the Decouds and the MacWhirrs? There is also Stein; and Emilia Gould, who thought: "Our daily work must be done to the glory of the dead, and for the good of those who come after."

Let us turn, at long last, to *Nostromo*, the novel. In this book Conrad endeavored to create a great, massive, multiphase symbol that would render his total vision of the world, his sense of individual destiny, his sense of man's place in nature, his sense of history and society.

First, *Nostromo* is a complex of personal stories, intimately interfused, a chromatic scale of attitudes, a study in the definition and necessity of "illusion" as Conrad freighted that word. Each character lives by his necessary idealization, up the scale from the "natural" man Nostromo, whose only idealization is that primitive one of his vanity, to Emilia Gould, who, more than any other, has purged the self and entered the human community.

The personal stories are related not only in the contact of person and person in plot and as carriers of variations of the theme of illusion, but also in reference to the social and historical theme. That is, each character is also a carrier of an attitude toward, a point of view about, society; and each is an actor in a crucial historical moment. This historical moment is presumably intended to embody the main issues of Conrad's time: capitalism, imperialism, revolution, social justice. Many of the personal illusions bear quite directly on these topics: Viola's libertarianism, with its dignity and leonine self-sufficiency and, even, contempt for the mob; Charles Gould's obsession in his mission; Avellanos's liberalism and Antonia's patriotic piety; Holroyd's concern with a "pure form of Christianity" which serves as a mask and justification for his imperialistic thirst for power; even the posturing and strutting "Caesarism" of Pedrito Montero, whose imagination had been inflamed by reading third-rate historical novels.

All readers of Conrad know the classic picture of imperialism at its brutal worst in *Heart of Darkness*, the degradation and insanity of the process, and remember the passage spoken by Marlow:

"The conquest of the earth, which mostly means the taking it away from those who have a different complexion or slightly flatter noses than ourselves, is not a pretty thing when you look into it too much. What redeems it is the idea only."

In *Heart of Darkness* we see the process absolutely devoid of "idea," with lust, sadism, and greed rampant. In *Nostromo* we see the imperialistic process in another perspective, as the bringer of order and law to a lawless land, of prosperity to a land of grinding poverty. At least, that is the perspective in which Charles Gould sees himself and his mine:

"What is wanted here is law, good faith, order, security. Anyone can declaim about these things, but I pin my faith to material interests. Only let the material interests once get a firm footing, and they are bound to impose the conditions on which alone they can continue to exist. That's how your money-making is justified here in the face of lawlessness and disorder. It is justified because the security which it demands must be shared with an oppressed people."

This passage and Gould's conception of his own role may be taken as the central fact of the social and historical theme of *Nostromo*. But how does Conrad intend us to regard this passage? Albert Guerard, Jr., in his careful and brilliant study of Conrad, says that the mine "corrupts Sulaco, bringing civil war rather than progress." That strikes me as far too simple. There has been a civil war but the forces of "progress"—i.e., the San Tomé mine and the capitalistic order—have won. And we must admit that the society at the end of the book is preferable to that at the beginning.

Charles Gould's statement, and his victory, are, however, hedged about with all sorts of ironies. For one thing—and how cunning is this stroke!—there is Decoud's narrative, the letter written to his sister in the midst of the violence, that appears at the very center of the book; and the voice of the skeptic tells us how history is fulfilled. For another thing—and this stroke is even more cunning—old Captain Mitchell, faithful-hearted and stupid, the courageous dolt, is the narrator of what he pleases to call the "historical events." His is the first human voice we have heard, in chapter 2 of part 1, after the mists part to exhibit the great panorama of the mountains, campo, city, and gulf; and in chapter 10 of part 3, just after Nostromo has made his decision to ride to Cayta and save the Concession and the new state, the voice of Captain Mitchell resumes. He is speaking long afterward, to some nameless distinguished visitor, and now all the violence and passion and the great anonymous forces of history come under the unconscious irony of his droning anecdotes. We can say of Captain Mitchell what Conrad says of Pedrito Montero, inflamed by his bad novels read in a Parisian garret: his mind is "wrapped . . . in the futilities of historical anecdote." Captain Mitchell's view is, we may say, the "official view": "Progress" has triumphed, the world has achieved itself, there is nothing left but to enjoy the fruits of the famous victory. Thus the very personalities of the narrators function as commentary (in a triumph of technical virtuosity) as their voices are interpolated into Conrad's high and impersonal discourse.

But we do not have to depend merely on this subtle commentary. Toward the end of the book, at a moment of pause when all seems to be achieved on a sort of Fiddler's Green at the end of history, a party has gathered in the garden of the Casa Gould. They discuss in a desultory way the possibility of a new revolution, and the existence of secret societies in which Nostromo, despite his secret treasure and growing wealth, is a great force. Emilia Gould demands: "Will there never be any peace?" And Dr. Monygham replies:

> "There is no peace and no rest in the development of material interests. They have their law and their justice. But it is founded on expediency, and is inhuman; it is without rectitude, and without the continuity and force that can be found only in a moral principle. Mrs. Gould, the time approaches when all that the Gould Concession stands for shall weigh as heavily upon the people as the barbarism, cruelty, and misrule of a few years back."

The material interests have fulfilled their historical mission, or are in the process of fulfilling it. Even Charles Gould, long before, in defining his mission to bring order through the capitalistic development, had not seen that order as the end, only as a phase. He had said: "A better justice will come afterwards. That's our ray of hope." And in this connection we may recall in *Under Western Eyes* how, after hearing the old teacher of languages give his disillusioned view of revolution, Miss Haldin can still say: "I would take liberty from any hand as a hungry man would snatch at a piece of bread. The true progress must begin after." In other words, the empire-builder and hard-bitten realist Gould and the idealistic girl join to see beyond the era of material interests and the era of revolution the time of "true progress" and the "better justice." Somewhere, beyond, there will be, according to Miss Haldin's version, the period of concord:

> I believe that the future will be merciful to us all. Revolutionist and reactionary, victim and executioner, betrayer and betrayed,

they shall all be pitied together when the light breaks on our black sky at last. Pitied and forgotten; for without that there can be no union and no love.

Emilia Gould, trapped in her "merciless nightmare" in the "Treasure House of the World," leans over the dying capataz and hears him say, "But there is something accursed in wealth." Then he begins to tell her where the treasure is hidden. But she bursts out: "Let it be lost for ever."

If in this moment of vision, Emilia Gould and (in a sense that we shall come to) Conrad himself repudiate the material interests as merely a step toward justice, what are we to make of revolution? We may remember that Conrad most anxiously meditated the epigraphs of his various books, and that the epigraph of *Nostromo* is the line from Shakespeare: "So foul a sky clears not without a storm." It is innocent to think that this refers merely to the "storm" which is the action of the novel, the revolution that has established the order of material interests in Sulaco. If the sky has cleared at the end of that episode, even now in the new peace we see, as Dr. Monygham sees, the blacker and more terrible thunderheads piling up on the far horizon.

Heart of Darkness and *Nostromo* are, in one sense, an analysis and unmasking of capitalism as it manifested itself in the imperialistic adventure. Necessarily this involves the topic of revolution. The end of *Nostromo* leaves the sky again foul, and in the years immediately after finishing that novel Conrad turns to two studies of revolution, *The Secret Agent*, begun in 1905 and published in 1907, and *Under Western Eyes*, begun in 1908 and published in 1911. These books are in their way an analysis and unmasking of revolution to correspond to the already accomplished analysis and unmasking of capitalism and imperialism. In the world of revolution we find the same complex of egotism, vanity, violence, and even noble illusion. As the old teacher of languages in *Under Western Eyes* puts it:

A violent revolution falls into the hands of the narrow-minded fanatics and of tyrannical hypocrites at first. Afterwards comes the turn of all the pretentious intellectual failures of the time. Such are the chiefs and the leaders. You will notice that I have left out the mere rogues. The scrupulous and the just, the noble, humane, and devoted natures; the unselfish and the intelligent may begin a movement—but it passes away from them. They are not the leaders of a revolution. They are its victims: the victims of disgust, of disenchantment—often of remorse. Hopes grotesquely betrayed, ideal caricatured—that is the definition of revolutionary success. There have been in every revolution hearts broken by such successes.

We could take this, in appropriate paraphrase, as a summary of the situation at the end of *Nostromo*. There is the same irony of success. There has been the same contamination of the vision in the very effort to realize the vision. As Emilia Gould reflects: "There was something inherent in the necessities of successful action which carried with it the moral degradation of the idea."

Man, however, is committed to action. The Heysts, who repudiate action, find their own kind of damnation. Wisdom, then, is the recognition of man's condition, the condition of the creature made without gills or fins but dropped into the sea, the necessity of living with the ever renewing dilemma of idea as opposed to nature, morality to action, "utopianism" to "secular logic" (to take Razumov's terms from *Under Western Eyes*), justice to material interests. Man must make his life somehow in the dialectical process of these terms, and in so far as he is to achieve redemption he must do so through an awareness of his condition that identifies him with the general human communion, not in abstraction, not in mere doctrine, but immediately. The victory is never won, the redemption must be continually re-earned. And as for history, there is no Fiddler's Green, at least not near and soon. History is a process fraught with risks, and the moral regeneration of society depends not upon shifts in mechanism but upon the moral regeneration of men. But nothing is to be hoped for, even in the most modest way, if men lose the vision of the time of concord, when "the light breaks on our black sky at last." That Platonic vision is what makes life possible in its ruck and confusion, if we are to take Conrad's word from the essay called "Books":

> I would require from him [the artist] many acts of faith of which the first would be the cherishing of an undying hope; and hope, it will not be contested, implies all the piety of effort and renunciation. It is the God-sent form of trust in the magic force and inspiration belonging to the life of this earth. We are inclined to forget that the way of excellence is in the intellectual, as distinguished from emotional, humility. What one feels so hopelessly barren in declared pessimism is just its arrogance. It seems as if the discovery made by many men at various times that there is much evil in the world were a source of proud and unholy joy unto some of the modern writers. That frame of mind is not the proper one in which to approach seriously the art of fiction. It gives an author—goodness only knows why—an elated sense of his own superiority. And there is nothing more dangerous than such an elation to that absolute loyalty towards his own feelings

and sensations an author should keep hold of in his most exalted moments of creation.

To be hopeful in an artistic sense it is not necessary to think that the world is good. It is enough to believe that there is no impossibility of its being made so.

Nothing, however, is easy or certain. Man is precariously balanced in his humanity between the black inward abyss of himself and the black outward abyss of nature. What Conrad meant by and felt about man's perilous balance must already be clear, if I can make it clear at all. But now I shall speak of *Nostromo* as an image of this.

The setting of the story, the isolation of Sulaco, is in itself significant. The serrated wall of the Cordillera, hieratic and snow-capped, behind the Campo, the Azuera and the Golfo Placido define a little world that comes to us as complete—as a microcosm, we may say, of the greater world and its history. Man is lost in this overwhelming scene. The story of the two gringos, spectral and alive, on the peninsula of Azuera is, of course, a fable of greed and of the terrifying logic of material interests unredeemed. But it is also a fable, here at the threshold of *Nostromo*, of man lost in the blankness of nature. At the center of the book, to resume the same theme, we find the story of Decoud, who loses his identity into the "world of cloud and water, of natural forces and forms of nature." When he commits suicide, he falls into the "immense indifference of things." Then at the very end of the novel, in the last paragraph, Dr. Monygham, in the police-galley, hears the wild, faithful cry uttered by Linda, the name of Nostromo: "Never! Gian' Battista!"

> It was another of Nostromo's successes, the greatest, the most enviable, the most sinister of all. In that true cry of love and grief that seemed to ring aloud from Punta Mala to Azuera and away to the bright line of the horizon, overhung by a big white cloud shining like a mass of solid silver, the genius of the magnificent Capataz de Cargadores dominated the dark gulf containing his conquests of treasure and love.

This, too, is a fable: the passionate cry in the night that is a kind of triumph in the face of the immense indifference of things. It is a fable with a moral not unlike that of the second of Yeats's "Two Songs from a Play":

> Whatever flames upon the night
> Man's own resinous heart has fed.

Or to take another fable, one from Conrad's essay on Henry James:

When the last aqueduct shall have crumbled to pieces, the last airship fallen to the ground, the last blade of grass have died upon a dying earth, man, indomitable by his training in resistance to misery and pain, shall set this undiminished light of his eyes against the feeble glow of the sun. . . .

For my own part, from a short and cursory acquaintance with my kind, I am inclined to think that the last utterance will formulate, strange as it may appear, some hope now to us utterly inconceivable.

I have tried to define my reading of Conrad's work in general and of *Nostromo* in particular. In these matters there is not, and should not be, an ultimate "reading." a final word and orthodoxy of interpretation. In so far as a work is vital, there will continually be a development, an extrapolation of significance. But at any one moment each of us must take the risk of his sensibility and his logic in making a reading. I have taken this risk, and part of this risk is the repudiation, or at least criticism, of competing interpretations.

There is one view, not uncommonly encountered, that Conrad did not intend his fiction to have "meaning." We encounter, for example, the comment of Edward Crankshaw: "Bothering about what Conrad meant in *Heart of Darkness* is as irrelevant as bothering about what Mozart meant in the Haffner Symphony." Conrad himself gives some support to this view in his skeptical bias, in his emphasis on the merely spectacular value of life, and in not a few of his remarks on his literary intentions, particularly in the famous one: "My task which I am trying to achieve is, by the power of the written word, to make you hear, to make you feel—it is, before all, to make you *see*."

All of this seems to me, however, to mean nothing more than that Conrad was an artist, that he wanted, in other words, to arrive at his meanings immediately, through the sensuous renderings of passionate experience, and not merely to define meanings in abstraction, as didacticism or moralizing. Conrad made no split between literature and life. If anything, he insisted on the deepest inward relationship. As he put it about the writer in the essay "Books": "It is in the impartial practice of life, if anywhere, that the promise of perfection for his art can be found, rather than in the absurd formulas trying to prescribe this or that particular method of technique or conception."

Over and over again, Conrad implies what he says in the Author's Note to *Chance*: "But every subject in the region of intellect and emotion must have a morality of its own if it is treated at all sincerely; and even the most artful writer will give himself (and his morality) away in about every third sentence." And even to the famous sentence about his intention being, before all, to make us "*see*," we find an addition: "That—and no more, and it is everything." To seeing in its fullest sense, to "our sympathetic imagination," as Conrad says in "Autocracy and War," we must look "for the ultimate triumph of concord and justice."

If in *A Personal Record* Conrad declares himself an "imperfect Esthete," in the same sentence he admits that he is "no better philosopher." Leavis goes so far as to affirm that Conrad cannot be said to have a philosophy: "He is not one of those writers who clear up their fundamental attitudes for themselves in such a way that we may reasonably, in talking of them, use that portentous term." In discussing this remark, as I am about to do, I run the risk of making Conrad's work seem too schematic and of implying that he somehow sat down and worked out a philosophy which he then projected, with allegorical precision, into fiction. I mean nothing of the sort, but I do mean to say that in my judgment Leavis takes Conrad's work as too much a casual matter of temperament. For I think that even if Conrad is as "imperfect" philosopher as aesthete, he is still, in the fullest sense of the term, a philosophical novelist.

The philosophical novelist, or poet, is one for whom the documentation of the world is constantly striving to rise to the level of generalization about values, for whom the image strives to rise to symbol, for whom images always fall into a dialectical configuration, for whom the urgency of experience, no matter how vividly and strongly experience may enchant, is the urgency to know the meaning of experience. This is not to say that the philosophical novelist is schematic and deductive. It is to say quite the contrary, that he is willing to go naked into the pit, again and again, to make the same old struggle for his truth. But we cannot better Conrad's own statement for the philosophical novelist, the kind of novelist he undertook, quite consciously, to be: "Even before the most seductive reveries I have remained mindful of that sobriety of interior life, that asceticism of sentiment, in which alone the naked form of truth, such as one conceives it, can be rendered without shame."

For him the very act of composition was a way of knowing, a way of exploration. In one sense this is bound to be true of all composition, but the matter of degree and self-consciousness is important in our present distinction, even crucial. We know a little of how *Nostromo* came to be, how it rose out of a feeling of blankness, how its composition was, in sober fact, an exploration and a growth, how the "great mirage," as Edward Garnett called it, took shape until it could float before us, vivid and severe, one of the few mastering visions of our historical moment and our human lot.

Guardianship of the Treasure: *Nostromo*

Dorothy Van Ghent

The subject of *Nostromo* is the guardianship of a treasure, a simple and fateful subject common throughout folklore. In this novel, the material form of the treasure is the silver of the San Tomé mine, in the republic of Costaguana, on the west coast of South America. The mine belongs, as a permanent concession, to the English family of Goulds; but successive civil wars, which have laid waste the land, have destroyed the workings of the mine. Charles Gould, an experienced mining engineer, sets out to rehabilitate it with the aid of North American capital. It becomes a financial success, and its success brings about the peace and order necessary for sustained economic enterprise. But when the main action of the story opens, a new political revolution, motivated by greed for the mine's riches, threatens the established order with bloodshed and anarchy.

Conrad's most fertile invention in *Nostromo* is to adapt the legendary idea of the mysterious potency of a treasure to the conditions of a frontier country in a modern period of colonial imperialism. In folklore a treasure is always a powerful *mana*-object that tests the characters of men; it confers great benefits, but only those with the highest physical and moral courage, and the deepest spiritual insight, are able to recognize its true nature and to use it properly. In a story with a modern milieu, the treasure can be quite concretely the chief industrial resource of a country—a rich silver mine—and yet, through the way men interpret its potential uses, it can arouse the most violent and disparate human responses, from crude appetite to passionate idealism. Actually, everybody in Conrad's story has a different attitude toward the silver of the mine. To some it is an opportunity for loot. To

From *Joseph Conrad: A Collection of Criticism*, edited by Frederick R. Karl. © 1975 by McGraw-Hill Publishers.

others, it is the material "fact" that has made legal security and good government possible—possible, at least, until revolution again threatens. To Charles Gould, it has a very personal meaning. His father had been forced by corrupt and impotent governments to pay ruinous royalties on the then worthless property, and had died from outrage at such a perversion of justice. Gould has come under the fascination of the idea that if he can make a success of the mine, it will be a "way of atonement" for his father's death. The development and protection of the mine are to him a moral necessity.

Part of the range of ambiguity in what the treasure of the mine signifies may be illustrated by those occasions when we see the silver ingots in somebody's hands. Mrs. Gould had received the first ingot from the reopened vein, and, in her devotion to her husband, the silver seemed to her to be the palpable expression of his idealism:

> she had seen the first spungy lump of silver yielded to the hazards of the world by the dark depths of the Gould Concession; she had laid her unmercenary hands, with an eagerness that made them tremble, upon the first silver ingot turned out warm from the mould; and by her imaginative estimate of its power she endowed that lump of metal with a justificative conception, as though it were not a mere fact, but something far-reaching and impalpable, like the true expression of an emotion or the emergence of a principle.

The Goulds have no children. It is suggested that, with a subtle unfaithfulness to his wife, Charles Gould has allowed his redemptory idea of the mine to usurp her place in his emotions. The language in the passage above is that of a birth, of "emergence" from "dark depths." The "spungy lump," "still warm from the mould," lies in Emilia Gould's hands as a "conception," a truly immaculate conception and the only one she will know. The San Tomé mine is to make her married life barren.

Nostromo, foreman of the stevedores who load the silver for shipping north, also is seen with ingots in his hands. Nostromo's name has come to stand for absolute fidelity and incorruptibility. But in the last episode of the story, he has become a thief. He steals a few ingots at a time from the bargeload of silver he has buried on a desert island, and disposes of them secretly so that his good name will be protected while he grows rich. To Nostromo, the treasure of the mine has meant moral death, and the touch of the ingots is hateful to him. They bear "the smell of earth, of damp foliage," the smell of a dark rot in nature.

Martin Decoud, the young Creole intellectual, is the third person who is seen in physical contact with the silver. To Decoud, the treasure has finally no more meaning than any other dead weight which will help a man to drown. He puts a couple of the heavy ingots in each pocket before he commits suicide in the Golfo Placido.

In even so slight a sketch, more than one major folklore element may be seen. There is not only the treasure itself—which in myth and fairy tale may be a golden fleece, the golden apples of the Hesperides, a horse or hound with supernatural powers, the Holy Grail, or other variations on the idea of a treasure. There is also, in the part played by Charles Gould, the motif of the "stranger knight" who comes to a "waste land," and who, because of his moral purity, is able to rehabilitate the land. Gould is always described as extremely foreign-looking, with his thin, blazingly red face and fiery moustaches; he comes from abroad (his youth was spent in Europe); he rescues the treasure of the land from the forces of corruption, and thereby brings about peace and prosperity. In a fairy tale, when the knight has accomplished his mission, he becomes the "good king" and reigns happily ever after. Gould is called the "king" of the province where the mine is located—El Rey de Sulaco. But he does not reign happily ever after. Apparently there was something wrong with his interpretation of the use of the treasure, for the same old troubles of corrupt intrigue, war, and widespread ruin appear again in the land.

In fairy tales where a treasure is the central emblem, a fairy princess is almost always associated with it, so closely that she may be looked upon as an essential part of the treasure itself. The "stranger knight's" marriage with the fairy princess is the crown of his successes. Their union is a traditional image of union and communion between people. The motif of marriage is one significant indication that the treasure in the fairy tale is more than a material thing; it is a thing with spiritual powers, and one of its mysterious significances is fulfillment in human communion. Several times Conrad describes Emilia Gould as "fairy-like," with her masses of fair hair, the rich rings on her fingers and lace on her wrists, "gracious, small, and fairy-like, before the glittering tea-set." The sterile relationship between Charles Gould and his wife is one of the important variations Conrad makes on a legendary model. This we shall examine a little more closely later.

All of the other people in *Nostromo* may be seen in terms of various tropisms of human desire when tested by the treasure—a treasure always ambiguous because it shows itself to the characters only in forms complementary to "the secret purposes of their hearts revealed amongst the bitter necessities of the time." The ordeal that each undergoes, when his deepest attitude toward the treasure is tested, forms the action of the novel.

The "ordeal" is a constant element of stories formed on the kind of model we are considering. Mortal dangers must be gone through by the adventurer who would win the benefits that a treasure can confer. This motif is found in the most sophisticated literature—like Conrad's *Nostromo* —as well as in naive folklore, simply because it represents the arduous necessities of man's work in fulfilling his needs and desires. It will be helpful to consider, in a rather simple fairy tale, the ordeal gone through by a character who desires to win a treasure, so that the complex action of Conrad's novel may be more readily grasped. The ancient Irish fairy tale about Conn-Eda will serve. In this tale, the ordeal has three phases (each phase is found also in Conrad's novel). The hero, who starts out pure of heart, must, before he can command the treasure and become the "good king," pass these three tests: he must face wisely and courageously the destructive forces of nature, the evil in other people, and the evil in himself.

The queen, Conn-Eda's mother, died. His father, the king, married another woman—wicked, as all stepmothers in fairy tales are wicked. The wicked stepmother laid the good and innocent young prince under a magic forfeit, by which he was obliged to go on a deadly journey to fairyland, to obtain a treasure there. Conn-Eda asked the advice of the animals, and was told to take a little shaggy horse and to follow a rolling iron ball. He trusts, that is, to instinct (the little shaggy horse) and the laws of nature (the iron ball follows the law of gravity). But Conn-Eda, though young and innocent, has physical discipline, and he is brave. When raging water-serpents attack him, he skillfully throws them chunks of meat which the little shaggy horse carries in his ears for such an emergency. When he has to cross a mountain of fire, he makes the terrible leap through the flames courageously, and though he is scorched nearly to death, the horse has a bottle of medicine in his ear that heals the wounds, and Conn-Eda manages to go on. His worst ordeal comes at the gates of fairyland, where the little shaggy horse tells him he must kill his faithful animal companion with a knife, if they are to avoid an even greater evil. Conn-Eda has learned the evil in people, from his wicked stepmother, and the destructiveness in nature, from the water-serpents and the fire-mountain; now he is required to learn the evil of which he himself is capable. He refuses, weeping, to kill his animal friend, but somehow the knife moves of itself in his hand, and the little horse lies dead. From its carcass springs a beautiful fairy prince. He helps Conn-Eda obtain the treasure and a fairy princess for his bride; the wicked stepmother falls dead from spite; and Conn-Eda's reign over his land is wise and just, the best in all Ireland.

The fairy prince who springs from the carcass of the shaggy horse can be interpreted metaphorically as representing Conn-Eda himself, after he has passed the ordeals and acquired from them the wisdom to rule. It is significant that Conn-Eda has both his father's and his mother's names—Conn and Eda; for in his nature he preserves both the humble, cherishing maternal principle, and the aggressive, rational paternal principle. Though he starts out innocent on his adventure, he has the humility to trust to instinct, such as the animals have; and he has the fortitude and discipline that a man must have to face the elemental forces of nature (that is why his wounds, though terrible, are again and again healed by the magic medicine). He wins, in the most difficult way, the experience necessary for the application of reason and for aggressive command, such as a king must have. But he is able, in the end, to integrate all of these qualities. "Reborn" from the ordeals of external evil and the deepest self-knowledge, he is now wise enough to become the guardian of the treasure of fairyland. The treasure of fairyland—the good of life, the goal of desire—is finally seen to be within and not without: it is the wisdom Conn-Eda has gained.

Let us trace the phases of the ordeal in *Nostromo*. Of evidently great importance in Conrad's design is the man Nostromo himself, who gives the title to the book, and whose name constantly occurs as leitmotif even when he is not in the foreground of the action: That Nostromo's character and role should have primary importance seems, at first glance, out of keeping with Conrad's habitual concern with subtle problems of conscience, for Nostromo does not have any subtlety of conscience to make him psychologically interesting in the way Conrad's principal characters usually are. He is called the "natural man," the "Man of the People," and his lack of a cultivated conscience is precisely the reason for his importance in this novel that is broadly representative of the human condition: for the great multitudes of men everywhere are without benefit of the cultivated conscience. Nostromo presents in clear relief the first and elemental phase of the human ordeal, the facing of the primitive tests of nature. His great achievements lie in the world of nature, which he can master because he is virile and brave and physically skillful. These Adamic qualities are implicit in the poetic image of his awakening after his swim from the sunken barge:

> Nostromo woke up from a fourteen-hours' sleep and arose full
> length from his lair in the long grass. He stood knee-deep among
> the whispering undulations of the green blades, with the lost air
> of a man just born into the world. Handsome, robust, and supple,
> he threw back his head, flung his arms open, and stretched him-
> self with a slow twist of the waist and a leisurely growling yawn

of white teeth; as natural and free from evil in the moment of waking as a magnificent and unconscious wild beast. Then, in the suddenly steadied glance fixed upon nothing from under a forced frown, appeared the man.

But the world in which Nostromo lives is not the Adamic world, "natural and free from evil." It is, rather, a frontier world, where a sleepy, pastoral Campo has been invaded by industrialism, bringing with it all the complex energies, confusion of racial histories and attitudes, and moral anxieties that an industrial revolution introduces to a pastoral colonial people. In this frontier setting, the natural tests of manhood are still vitally necessary, and Nostromo passes these valiantly—tests of the sea and the mountains, and those which give a man command over the primitive passions and appetites of other men. But, tragically, ability to pass these tests is not enough.

Nostromo's superb natural gifts have their "ideal" and summary form in the virtue of fidelity—the virtue that relates him ethically to other men. But the men to whom he is bound in fidelity are men who belong to the invading industrial front—the San Tomé mine, the North American silver and iron interests, the European shipping and railway interests that have made capital investments in Costaguana. These men are involved in a vastly complicated enterprise whose potential for either good or evil is beyond the understanding of the "natural man," who has only instinct and virile pride to guide him. When revolutionary anarchy threatens the industrial interests, Nostromo is entrusted with a silver shipment, to be taken out to sea and beyond the reach of the rioters in the city. It is his great ordeal, the most "desperate affair" of his life, and he gives to it all his courage, all his skill, all his fidelity. But, afterwards, he learns that, in the complication of events, it actually mattered very little whether the silver was saved or whether it sank to the bottom of the sea. Nostromo had risked his life for nothing; his fidelity had meant nothing. His sense of the meaning of his own identity is completely baffled, for it has been undervalued by the men to whom he was faithful. Only the silver remains as a palpable fact to be trusted. Faithful to the silver, Nostromo becomes a thief.

He dies with "the bewildered conviction of having been betrayed"—as Adam himself, emerged without preparation out of the simple garden of nature into the human world of sin and death, must have died with the same sense of having been betrayed and "hardly knowing by what or by whom." The other figures in the novel, all caught in the "bitter necessities" of the frontier state, gain their plastic, significant relief from Nostromo's presence, the presence of the "natural man" whose primitive endowments are the base for any more evolved morality. Therefore his name is uttered again and again, as that of the "indispensable man" upon whom all the other characters are dependent in one way or another. Pacing slowly on his silver-grey mare through the night streets, his face muffled mysteriously by his sombrero, he is the man in the background, whose ancestry is older than civilization, and who has not even a proper kind of Christian name.

Charles Gould has his own unquestionable courage, his skill as a mining engineer, and his authority in commanding men to his purpose. But he also has, as Nostromo has not, an understanding of the complexities of the frontier milieu where he has to do his work. To return to our fairy-tale paradigm, the actions of Gould correspond with that phase of the human ordeal which demands experience of psychological evil in others in order that the treasure of life may be understood and properly used. And yet, as with Nostromo, Gould's particular gifts are not by themselves enough.

"Charles Gould was competent because he had no illusions," we are told. Nobody could be more aware of the murderous anarchism in Costaguana politics. One of his uncles had been elected President of the province of Sulaco and afterwards was put up against a wall and shot. His father had inculcated in him since childhood his own experience of the greed and corruption of Costaguana officials, the same type of officials with whom Gould has to deal in running the mine. He is also under no illusion about the motives of the North American financier who has made the working of the mine possible, the great Holroyd, the millionaire endower of churches, who expresses his faith in American capitalism this way:

> We shall be giving the word for everything—industry, trade, law, journalism, art, politics, and religion, from Cape Horn clear over to Smith's Sound, and beyond, too, if anything worth taking hold of turns up at the North Pole. And then we shall have the leisure to take in hand the outlying islands and continents of the earth. We shall run the world's business whether the world likes it or not. The world can't help it—and neither can we, I guess.

But Gould is not fooled into collaboration with anyone else's vast conceptions of destiny. The success of the San Tomé mine is an aim which is "definite in space and absolutely attainable within a limited time," and it makes the other man, Holroyd, with his "insatiable imagination of conquest," appear "as a dreamy idealist of no importance." Gould's experience prepares him to stoop for his weapons, both in using Holroyd's millions to get the mine working, and in dealing with Costaguana politicians and racketeers.

He stakes his character on the success of the mine; his moral identity is bound up with it. In this way, he feels that he has kept his own personal motive pure and independent—the motive of "atonement" for his father's death by redemption of the mine that had killed his father. For "material interest" alone he would not have touched the mine, but "material interests" have made success possible, and vaguely he recognizes certain social ideals that may be fulfilled along the way. "What is wanted here is law, good faith, order, security," he tells his wife.

> Only let the material interests once get a firm footing and they are bound to impose the conditions on which alone they can continue to exist. That's how your money-making is justified here in the face of lawlessness and disorder. It is justified because the security which it demands must be shared with an oppressed people. A better justice will come afterwards. That's your ray of hope.

But all this—law and order, good faith, security and justice for an oppressed people—is merely incidental to Gould's personal obsession, and his sense of the sacrosanct purity of his own private intention has itself prevented him from submitting to the final ordeal of self-knowledge. His idea of father-atonement is a kind of adultery, subtly wooing him away from his wife, who is left in the isolation of a sterile marriage. At moments he seems dimly aware of this fact, but emotionally unable to face it:

> He bent over her upturned face very tenderly and a little re-morsefully. . . . For a moment he felt as if the silver-mine, which had killed his father, had decoyed him farther than he meant to go; and with the round-about logic of emotions, he felt that the worthiness of his life was bound up with success. There was no going back.

In the legendary terms that we have been using to clarify the emble-matic aspects of the novel, what Gould fails to recognize is that the "trea-sure" is worthless without the "fairy princess," and that in abusing his union with her he has refused the human communion that is an essential benison of the treasure. In his abstract, obsessional commitment to the father, he has lost touch with the feminine, maternal principle which cherishes for its own sake—as Emilia Gould does—"the past and the future in every passing moment of the present."

Dr. Monygham's part in the book corresponds with the third phase of the ordeal—that of self-knowledge. Long before the main action of the story starts, Dr. Monygham has suffered the experience of evil in himself—an experience analogous to that moment in the tale of Conn-Eda when the prince is called upon to kill his best friend, the little shaggy horse, and though he refuses to do so, finds that the knife nevertheless moves in his hand and the deed is done. In the time of the bloody dictator, Guzman Bento, Monygham had been tortured and confessions were extorted from him implicating some of his best friends, who were imprisoned and executed on that accusation. He bears testimony to his experience by the cicatrices on his cheeks, his damaged ankles and crooked feet. This battered personality, limping around Sulaco, has come under the spell of Emilia Gould—of "the delicate preciousness of her inner worth, partaking of a gem and a flower" —and the latent tenderness of his essentially loyal nature has unfolded to it. Whereas Charles Gould has abandoned his wife to loneliness because of his conviction that the "worthiness of his life" is bound up with the success of the mine, Dr. Monygham's sense of the *unworthiness* of his life leads him to an act of self-sacrifice by which he hopes to save Emilia Gould from a frightful disaster. In terms of our legendary model, Monygham, having learned by the ordeal of self-knowledge the helpless evil of which he is capable, has the humility to offer his life for another—and he offers it for the "fairy princess" who lives by giving herself wholly to others.

He deliberately adopts the character of a traitor. When menaces close around the mine—and not the least of these is Gould's decision to dynamite it sky-high to prevent it from falling into the hands of the revolutionary troops—he decoys a whole army out into the harbor, with the lie that Gould has sunk some of the silver there, for his own use, to be retrieved later by divers. The doctor is kept on the boat, with a noose around his neck, ready for hanging if the silver is not discovered. It is an act in which his damaged reputation serves him well, for the colonel of the army believes that Monygham would naturally betray Gould for a part of the loot. As the doctor tells himself, in bitter memory of his earlier ordeal, "I am the only one fit for that dirty work." But his ruse succeeds in relieving the besieged city.

In one way or another, for every character, the silver of the mine formulates the heart's "secret purposes," by the ordeal which each undergoes in relation to it. In Martin Decoud's case, we have something that escapes direct legendary parallel, except in an interpretive and revisionary way. What Decoud suffers may be "the greatest evil of all," which, in the Conn-Eda tale, the little shaggy horse says will befall both him and the prince if the prince refuses to take up the knife. The greatest evil of all is lack of faith in the treasure. If the treasure is the good of life, then lack of faith in it is death.

When Decoud is alone with the barge-load of silver on the Great Isabel, one of the sterile spurs of rock in the Golfo Placido, he discovers the "secret purpose" of his heart to be death. The principle of his life has been rationalism, the nineteenth- and twentieth-century heritage from the Enlightenment. For traditional rationalism, ultimate reality is the evidence of the senses, which is the raw material upon which reason works. What can reason do with the evidence of the senses, even with a pile of silver ingots beside one, on a desert island in the middle of an immense gulf where no ship passes? The Ancient Mariner had a similar problem:

> Alone, alone, all, all alone,
> Alone on a wide, wide sea!
> And never a saint took pity on
> My soul in agony.

One's senses, and what reason can make of them, become as indifferent as the sea and the sky and the rock and the silver itself. Decoud commits suicide in "the immense indifference of things."

Given the range of powerful ambiguities in the meaning of the "treasure," the opening chapter, with its purely geographic and atmospheric description of setting—the gulf of ocean, the towering Cordillera, the vast plain of the Campo, a telescopic glimpse of the town—gains profound significance. As the human action of the story is elemental, in the sense that it shows the basic patterns of human desire and endeavor, so also the setting is elemental, and is presented in the first chapter in a great hour-by-hour review as the earth makes its diurnal turning. The story is subtitled "A Tale of the Seaboard": it takes place at the edge of the sea and at the edge of the land, both of them in a perspective of immensity, under the unvarying cyclical changes of the infinite sky, of day and night; and the town itself, where the human events take place, seems very small in this perspective—Conrad gives it a single mention in the last line of the chapter. The physical vantage point from which the scene is viewed is the middle of the Golfo Placido, presumably on a ship approaching the harbor of Sulaco, and the view is dominated by the gulf—its cavernous vastness, the strange calms that prevail there because of the peninsular land masses enclosing it, its isolation from the more accessible trading points on the coast. Shadow, cloud, and mist keep moving out from the land over the water: at dawn, the great shadow of the Cordillera lies over it; at midday the clouds start rolling out from the valleys and the Cordillera itself disappears as if dissolved; at night the clouds smother the gulf in impenetrable darkness. As one approaches land, the Sulaco plain extends before one endlessly, overhung by dry haze, "an opal mystery of great distances." The description covers, at a precise location on the coast of South America, a twenty-four hour review of the major geographic and cosmic phenomena by which all life on the earth is oriented.

The chief dramatic action, on which are pivoted the destinies of all the characters, also takes place during a single twenty-four hour period: the night of the loading of the silver shipment to get it away from the revolutionary rioters, the dead of night with Nostromo and Decoud on the barge with the silver out in the gulf, sunset the next day and Nostromo's wakening at the old fort after swimming across the gulf, evening and his reappearance in Sulaco—and meanwhile, that same day in Sulaco, the arrival of revolutionary forces by sea, the imprisoning and questioning of Dr. Monygham as to the whereabouts of the silver, his decision to seduce the troops out of the city in search of buried plunder, and his meeting that evening with Nostromo when he persuades him to ride over the mountains for help. The book is concerned primarily with spiritual action—with the revelation, in the midst of ordeal, of the "secret purposes" in the hearts of the characters—but the ordeal itself is the dramatized action, for it is in dramatic action that the "secret purposes" are revealed. This action is temporally placed in a twenty-four hour unit of the cosmic cycle that is simply and powerfully sketched by Conrad in the first chapter as an endlessly repeated movement in the "mystery of great distances" by which human life is environed. The cosmic repetition reflects on the human events its own repetitive form, by which these events are seen as themselves eternal patterns of man's desire and endeavor.

As the dramatic action of the book is correlated with cosmic law, apprehended in the unvarying cycles of nature, so the "treasure"—the good that men seek—is correlated with spiritual law, operating in the human heart. The treasure reveals itself only as the heart interprets it. It judges the heart. Thus the strange calms of the Golfo Placido, its isolation as a place of destiny, the clouds and shadow, the luminous mists and haze, real and local as they are in time and place, are touches of the mystery that is both the human heart and the external spaces surrounding it.

In the second chapter, Conrad uses the leisurely drone of Captain Joseph Mitchell, head of the steamship post in Sulaco, to introduce sketchily the day of the riot—that day when the revolutionaries first threatened Sulaco, making it urgent that the silver of the mine, piled up in the steamship warehouse for shipment north, be loaded secretly at night and sent off —but Mitchell is telling about it years after the event. The accents are shifted, as it is pieced out in Mitchell's somewhat senile recollection. The reader scarcely apprehends what the riot was about, or that it has much importance for the novel. Overlaid by the passage of time, it is reduced now to a not very clear and—to all appearances—not very important local anecdote. This effect of temporal passage is a correlative of the great cyclical review, as of a planet turning, that the first chapter has given. There the setting of the drama was revolved in cosmic space, under the aspect of eternal repetition. Here, under the linear reduction of time, the effect is inverted and ironic.

Captain Mitchell's discourse is a device of temporal displacement to contrive varying and multiple perspectives on the action, and this device is used all through part 1 and most of part 2. It is only toward the end of part 2, with the letter Decoud writes to his sister on the day of the riot, that the main action of the book begins to emerge fully into the foreground. It may be that a reader would best approach the novel by starting with Decoud's letter and reading on to the end of part 2 (the night on the barge, the landing of Decoud and Nostromo on the Great Isabel), then returning to the beginning to read straight through. This suggestion will undoubtedly be unwelcome to scholars of Conrad who are concerned primarily with the "impressionistic" technique of the book. But *Nostromo* is a notoriously baffling novel to "get into," and technique can have little importance to readers who are so put off by the deviousness of the first chapters that they fail to read the book at all. Furthermore, novels of this order have a perennial vitality to which no harm can be done even if they are read backwards rather than forwards; and it may be that *Nostromo* is one of those books that profit by being read the first time middle-against-both-ends. This way, at least, one gets a more immediate grasp of the central events, which helps one to understand and evaluate more readily the shifting background of history and personal involvement which the first half of the book builds up.

Chapters 3 and 4 perform one of Conrad's wonderful modulations from vast space to intensely immediate visual detail, which make one understand more truly what he meant by saying that his task was "before all, to make you *see* . . . no more, and it is everything." The old Garibaldino, Giorgio Viola, is seen in his house—the inn named for Italian unity, "L'Italia Una"—with his wife Teresa and their two adolescent daughters. It is the day of the riot. The old warrior Giorgio is on guard; Signora Teresa sits bowed over her two girls; the windows are shuttered, there are sounds of sporadic tumult in the town, shooting, then intervals of unaccountable still-ness; they are tense, waiting for Nostromo—for this family, too, is depen-dent on Nostromo's courage and skill, as everyone in Sulaco is. Then they hear what they know to be the sound of a horse's shoulder scraped against a shutter, for a broad area of the pencil-lines of sunlight is effaced. It is Nostromo.

> Giorgio, with tranquil movements, had been unfastening the door; the flood of light fell on Signora Teresa, with her two girls gathered to her side, a picturesque woman in a pose of maternal exaltation. Behind her the wall was dazzlingly white, and the crude colors of the Garibaldi lithograph glowed in the sunshine.

This picture is done with simple sculptural modeling, using—as Conrad has a specially keen interest in using—effects of lighting against deep shadow, to make one "see" in the optical sense, which is preliminary to any more complicated modes of seeing. The language is not very nuanced: "a pic-turesque woman in a pose of maternal exaltation" is generalized phrasing for the abstractly "picture-like" and "sculpture-like"; but it is functional phrasing for the image that is needed, which is an impersonal, "classical" kind of image. For this is a classical kind of family, and through them a classical typology is achieved that deepens and strengthens the comprehen-sive human perspective in which events in Costaguana are placed.

They are classical as almost any Italian peasant family seems to be classical, in looks, in stances and gestures, in the career of their passions. (At the end of the book, a "classical" tragedy occurs in this family, combining incest with the murder of foster-son by father.) The classical type of the Viola family is set up beside the type of the "natural man," Nostromo—whose lineage, Conrad says, is "more ancient still," for he has "the weight of countless generations behind him and no parentage to speak of . . . like the People." Whereas the classical Viola family represents a traditional re-sponse to life in terms of a fully formed, complete, and unchanging set of mores (a response that is actually, therefore, anachronous on this unstable frontier), Nostromo, as the "natural man," has no cultural base, no estab-lished set of attitudes to put him into moral relationship, whether positive or negative, with a new frontier civilization that is itself unsteady, ambiguous, inwardly disorganized. Still another contrasting perspective is achieved be-tween old Giorgio's idealistic republicanism and the corruption and out-lawry of the Costaguanan revolutionaries on this day of the riot—a mob of thieves and demagogues shouting the bloodied words of political idealism. Giorgio's republicanism is itself classical—he is a man of the "old abstract revolutions," when men suffered not for gain but "for love of all humanity."

From the vivid detail of these two chapters, Conrad modulates back to the vast panoramic setting, now of mountain and plain, and one is given a first distant view of the actual physical violence of the Costaguana revolution—the somber and amorphous underground of the action of the book. Giorgio is standing at the door of the inn, curiously, watching the plain, where the horsed rioters are stumbling in their confused and meaningless battles:

> Tall trails of dust subsided here and there. In a speckless sky the sun hung clear and blinding. Knots of men ran headlong; others made a stand; and the irregular rattle of fire-arms came rippling to his ears in the fiery, still air. Single figures on foot raced desperately. Horsemen galloped towards each other, wheeled round together, separated at speed. Giorgio saw one fall, rider and horse disappearing as if they had galloped into a chasm, and the movements of the animated scene were like the peripeties of a violent game played upon the plain by dwarfs mounted and on foot, yelling with tiny throats, under the mountain that seemed a colossal embodiment of silence.

It is like a battle scene out of Paolo Uccello, crowded with lances and banners and the enormous rumps of horses, all utterly and frightfully static, for the feudal battles that Uccello painted were not battles—nobody but the horses got killed—but baronial trade markets in horseflesh, armorial banners, and hardware. So this scene of revolutionary riot, passing before the eyes of the old republican soldier, is given by the short rigid phrases a peculiarly small and static fury, for its deadly violence is also that of the horseflesh-and-hardware market.

The mindless greed and ferocity of the revolutionaries are the roiling of the abyss, the demonic underground, of this *comédie humaine*. The ordeals of the principal characters are played out on hierarchic levels, and the lowest level of all is the dark and tumultuous pit of human demonism, whose uproar is also released by desire for the "treasure." As in Dante's *Commedia*, certain monsters domineer over the abyss—like the *"gran bestia"* General Montero, military idol of the revolution, imbecile and ominous as some Aztec deity, awaiting with great flatulent nostrils the homage of the smoke of burned houses and the smell of spilled blood. Here also is that abject and random victim of the silver mine, Señor Hirsch, who had his own modest pecuniary deal to make for a part of the treasure, and who, in his blind and appalling cowardice, is unwittingly carried out to sea on a barge loaded with it. Señor Hirsch is finished off by the strapado, his senseless body leaping convulsively to the lash of the whip "like a fish on the end of a line"—an image of bestiality suitable to the gross dehumanization of the underground.

It is because of the primitive threat of the abyss, where appetite, fear, and passion rage without control, that the grave simple virtues of courage and fidelity are so important in the book. There is need for staunch guardians of the city, the mine, the villages where the mine workers live, and the poor Indios of the Campo. The men who have this role wear the marks of old and fierce campaigns on their bodies—men like General Barrios, with a grotesque black patch over his eye, and Father Corbelán, whose scarred cheeks suggest "something unlawful behind his priesthood, the idea of a chaplain of bandits." Like Nostromo, these men are brave, but unlike Nostromo, they serve the traditional functions of the military and the church; their fidelity is grounded in their profession, and does not run the subjective risk that Nostromo's does. Nostromo, alone in the book, is a tragic figure, thrown with full force on a personal destiny, in which the essential choice of his manhood is enacted in opposition to a mysterious historical necessity beyond his comprehension. As the "natural man," his is the tragic figure of mankind, facing the ambiguities of history with no equipment but the instinct of survival and the pride of being a man.

And yet, despite the tragic view of life that the book contains, it is a "comedy." It is a comedy in the Dantean and the Balzacian sense, signifying a drama in which all the representative forms of human action are shown as recurrent and resurgent, played out on a cosmic scene that stretches from the abyss of demonic egoism to the angelic level of selfless communion. Nobody really achieves the "treasure," that integration of virtue and wisdom which gives command of the good of life, for this is historical realism and not emblematic legend. Even Dr. Monygham is the slave of his own experience, which he has separated unnaturally from the ordeals of other men. Emilia Gould, who represents the highest benison of the treasure, is the most lonely person in the book, for her gift is the hardest of all to recognize.

Unlike gold—which corresponds alchemically to the sun's fire, the light of day and reason—silver is a nocturnal metal, correspondent to the moon, to emotion and imagination. The "treasure," whose emblem is silver, is misprized if it is thought to be any abstract ideal or truth (as Charles Gould thought it to be), or any theory of history that one might try to find in the story. The book shows on a vast scale the recurrence of the human ordeal and the resurgence of desire. It ends in moonlight, the brilliance of the moon lying like a bar of silver on the horizon, and with a cry of faith into the night.

Continuities and Discontinuities: *Middlemarch* and *Nostromo*

George Levine

In life, it is the present moment, the present fact, which is important; the moment which preceded, the facts which went before it, borrow all their interest from their relation to it. The mind, indeed, must "look before and after," but it stands upon the "now" and the "fact" with which it has to deal. We are but too apt, in our impatience, to neglect the present moment, casting longing glances backward on the days that are gone, and longing glances forward to the days that are to come, as if the former had not been, and the latter will not be, simple presents. We fail thus to enjoy the present, and to estimate the event or the man that is with us; we let the irrecoverable opportunity slip by, to regret it when it is gone.

    —G. H. LEWES, *Problems of Life and Mind*

Every moment some form grows perfect in hand or face; some tone on the hills or the sea is choicer than the rest; some mood of passion or insight or intellectual excitement is irresistibly real and attractive to us—for that moment only.
    —WALTER PATER, Conclusion to *The Renaissance*

To arrest, for the space of a breath, the hands busy about the work of the earth, and compel men entranced by the sight of distant goals to glance for a moment at the surrounding vision of form and colour, of sunshine and shadows; to make them pause for a look, for a sigh, for a smile—such is the aim, difficult and evanescent, and reserved only for a few to achieve.
    —JOSEPH CONRAD, Preface to *The Nigger of the "Narcissus"*

The three quotations in the epigraph to this chapter, one from a scientific treatise, one from a book about art, one from the preface to a novel, may suggest something of the community of vision amid the most disparate

From *The Realistic Imagination: English Fiction from Frankenstein to Lady Chatterley*. © 1981 by the University of Chicago. The University of Chicago Press, 1981.

enterprises and attitudes created by the diffusion of scientific knowledge in the last quarter of the nineteenth century. Lewes, who is in fact urging moral ardor, sounds like an aesthete. Pater, accused of decadent aestheticism, is also proposing a way to live, a moral program. Conrad, like the others intensely aware of the glory of the moment, of its transience, of the difficulty of focusing upon it, writes a liberating literary manifesto that seeks community in the particular. Between the George Eliot who was ironic alike about the nearsighted and about the farsighted, and the Conrad who struggled to find meaning in the immediate moment, there is a continuity and community of attitudes that persist through all the radical differences. The moment had become less stable, yet more important. Firmness of conviction and of idea had to give way before the wonder of immediate experience.

The distance between *Middlemarch* and *Nostromo* is thus by no means absolute. Seen together, in the light of the tradition I have tried to sketch in [*The Realistic Imagination*], they can provide a focal point for a last look at the transformation of the conventions of Victorian realism and of the moral aesthetic into the materials of modernism. (Ironically, there are even irrelevant connections between George Eliot and Conrad, as for example, that the Blackwood firm thought of Conrad's *Youth* as "the most notable book we have published since George Eliot.") *Middlemarch* and *Nostromo* are the most ambitious enterprises of their pseudonymous and late-blooming authors; separated by thirty-two years, they are both encyclopedic "histories" and imaginative articulations of the late-century scientific vision, the one still hopeful about the possibilities of discovery, the other more than disenchanted. While *Middlemarch* attempts to see the ideal in the real and charges each moment with the significances of multiple perspectives, *Nostromo* sees the real in the ideal while multiplying perspectives beyond the possibility of significance.

The case for seeing these books as discontinuous and not comparable is made most lucidly by Edward Said. (Although his reference is actually to *War and Peace*, his arguments are surely meant for books like *Middlemarch*, also.) His three main reasons are that "*Nostromo* aspires to no authority on matters of history and sociology"; it does not "create a normative world that resembles our own"; it is "assuredly not the product of a great established literature." But unless we take *Nostromo* as a completed assertion rather than as a process in "the remorseless rush of time," and disregard the tortuous narrative, it is misleading to claim that the novel does not "aspire" to authority. That it fails to achieve authority does not absolutely distinguish it from *Middlemarch*, a novel almost equally engaged with the problem, which yet struggles to find a language for a rapidly diffusing reality, and which leaves the issue almost as problematic as at the start.

Under the scrutiny to which modernist critics subject it, *Middlemarch* begins to look remarkably unstable and "unauthoritative." Relationships in it turn out to be extremely difficult to define precisely, without something like the artificial conditions of scientific experiment, with microscopes, shifts of perspective, controls. If it seems to adhere to the convention of chronological sequence, the chronology is greatly complicated by multiplications of narratives, by retrospects that "account for" the present moments, and by carefully contrived echoes and parallels among the divergent narratives. Scientific control is both artificial and elusive; for *Middlemarch* to achieve authority, as I think we are expected to believe Dorothea achieves it in her assistance to Lydgate at the end, it must leap beyond the calculable and controllable.

The distinction between the two texts is further blurred by the idea of the "normative." Although the very title of *Middlemarch* suggests a world that "resembles our own," the book encompasses an extreme, almost Dantean, imagination of the world, by which the surface of realism is informed with a mythic energy. Midway in our life's journey, we descend into a kind of hell; the "normative" world turns out to be filled with vampiric relations, Faustian overreachers, voices from beyond the grave. Conversely, the conventions that govern the geographically remote world of Costaguana are those of folktales or romantic adventures, but *Nostromo* reasserts the normative in the midst of extremes: it builds, like *Middlemarch*, a recognizable community within which dwell capitalists, industrialists, petty officials, hostelers, dockworkers, journalists, traders, and peasants. And if we expect extremes under *Nostromo's* tropical sun, it comes as a shock how much violence, psychological and physical, is incorporated in the little world of *Middlemarch*: murders, riots, blackmail and briberies, political rhetoric, deaths. Moreover, at a moral center of both books there is an inescapable analogy between Charles Gould, making his silver bear the burden of the ideological as he succumbs to its material power, and Nicholas Bulstrode, justifying his wealth by providence, and killing to preserve it.

There are enough such possible parallels to suggest a similarity in the raw materials of the two novels. Both are large historical fictions that attempt to create entire societies and—in the established tradition of Walter Scott—to read the fates of characters in the context of larger social and national movements from which they cannot withdraw. Both are preoccupied not only with Said's "authority" in personal, political, and literary senses, but with the relation among "feeling," idea, and action, with the way skepticism impedes, but is a condition of, intelligent action. As multiple perspectives layer and qualify each experience, history—even in *Middlemarch*—seems strangely unprogressive and nonchronological. In *Middlemarch*, the universe becomes a "tempting range of relevancies," full of connections too subtle for ordinary consciousness. As Lewes was writing at roughly the same time in *Problems of Life and Mind*: "Every Real is the complex of so many relations, a conjunction of so many sensations, that to know one Real thoroughly could only be possible through an intuition embracing the universe." A struggle for such an intuition seems to mark the achronology of *Nostromo*, where true connections remain yet more obscure.

I am not discussing similarity in order to argue identity. Nor am I claiming any direct influence (though it would be surprising if Conrad had not read *Middlemarch*). Literary history is a complex of continuities and discontinuities, rarely more than in the implicit history that connects and disconnects these two novels. The facile compartmentalization of "modern" and "old-fashioned" cannot suffice. Recent emphasis in criticism on originality, newness, or belatedness has its uses, and it is particularly useful to imagine, as Said's analysis requires, the absoluteness of all beginnings: "With regard to what precedes it, a beginning represents . . . a discontinuity." But discontinuity is comprehensible only in terms of some posited continuity, and both of these novels, although again they might fail, are self-consciously searching for "origins" in the context of scientific thought that was making origins unthinkable.

Middlemarch, for example, represents a continuity: it marks, as Henry James put it, "a limit to the development of the old-fashioned novel." But it is also a beginning, particularly of the self-conscious attempt to imagine a secular-scientific community in a world cut off from traditional continuities implied by earlier fictions. Conversely, *Nostromo* is impelled by an explanatory energy to overcome the discontinuities of its style. Why, otherwise, are there so many attempts to make clear when each event took place (e.g., "rather more than a year later"; "a year and a half later")? Why do we return to various actions to fill out our sense of what actually happened, as with the wonderful chapter describing Decoud's suicide, an event about which the primary fact is its absolute solitude? Who but a desperately explaining narrator could know or let us know about it? Alert to the literary conventions they can no longer sustain, both novels struggle within the realist tradition that seeks to get beyond literature into the real, now to confront the large threats of a universe latently hostile, monstrous and inhuman. One aspect of *Nostromo*'s narrative is its effort to make itself continuous with the tradition to which *Middlemarch* is so closely allied; it makes what we might call a "final" gesture at the possibility of registering the real within conventions of representation that *Middlemarch* itself calls into question.

Revelation and Repression in Conrad's *Nostromo*

Kiernan Ryan

> *The inner truth is hidden — luckily, luckily.*
> *—Heart of Darkness*

No really satisfactory account of *Nostromo* can, I think, begin to emerge without recognizing how the whole novel is produced and informed by a radical contradictory dynamic pulsing at the core of all Conrad's major fiction. Arnold Kettle raised the problem of the text's conflicting impulses some thirty years ago in *An Introduction to the English Novel*. On the one hand, as he points out, *Nostromo* powerfully and clearly pursues its uncompromising "moral discovery" of corruption and dehumanization in a society developing within the matrix of imperialism. Yet, at the same time, there is "a certain mistiness . . . buried deep in the language and symbolism of the book" and "there are moments in the novel when a sense of 'the cruel futility of things' does seem to overcome Conrad," a sense "that something in the very nature of things, something beyond human control (yet never defined), is responsible for the tragedy of *Nostromo*."

This perception of a fundamental contradictory tension troubling *Nostromo* has not, however, been confronted and thought through. Instead, criticism has oscillated between interpretations centred on only one main tendency of the novel at the expense of the other. *Nostromo* is construed as an essentially straightforward realist novel providing a solid representation and critique of a transparently intelligible social reality: "the essence of the

---

From *The Uses of Fiction: Essays on the Modern Novel in Honor of Arnold Kettle*, edited by Douglas Jefferson and Graham Martin. ©1982 by the Open University Press.

novel's meaning [is] that progress, leashed to faith in material interests, is inhuman, without rectitude, continuity, or force." And from within this critical perspective it can be affirmed that "there is nothing nihilistic about this 'Tale of the Seaboard.'" An opposing critical tendency, however, is concerned precisely to stress the nihilistic nature of *Nostromo*, its despairing, ironic vision of life as a meaningless illusion. This is the metaphysical version of Conrad epitomized by J. Hillis Miller's account, a version whose most recent avatars have produced an ultra-modernist *Nostromo* for which the impossibility of rendering reality at all, the problem of writing as such, is the real concern of an intensely reflexive text:

> Instead of mimetically authoring a new world, *Nostromo* turns back to its beginning as a novel, to the fictional, illusory assumption of reality; in thus overturning the confident edifice that novels normally construct *Nostromo* reveals itself to be no more than a *record* of novelistic self-reflection . . . a revulsion from the novelist's whole procreative enterprise and an intensification of his *scriptive* fate.
>
> (Edward Said, *Intention and Method*)

What is the exact nature of the text capable of producing such radically divergent interpretations? Conrad himself, significantly, can be cited in support of either critical emphasis. There is the strong, confident Conrad who sees his art as "a single-minded attempt to render the highest kind of justice to the visible universe by bringing to light the truth, manifold and one, underlying its every aspect"; whose task is "by the power of the written word to make you hear, to make you feel—it is, before all, to make you *see*" (Preface to *The Nigger of the "Narcissus"*). But then too there is the artistically paralyzed, agonizing Conrad before whom that "visible universe" dissolves into a meaningless void, its truth utterly beyond hope of communication:

> Even writing to a friend—to a person one has heard, touched, drank with, quarrelled with—does not give me a sense of reality. All is illusion—the words written, the mind at which they are aimed, the truth they are intended to express, the hands that will hold the paper, the eyes that will glance along the lines. Every image floats vaguely in a sea of doubt—and the doubt itself is lost in an unexplored universe of incertitudes.

We need to face the fact of a *constitutional* contradiction at the heart of Conrad's artistic vision and production of meaning. Criticism which suppresses this recognition in the recuperative quest for a unitary, harmonized version of Conrad severely distorts the contradictory character of his texts. Thus the unperturbed, straightforward "realist" readings of *Nostromo* are compelled to evade, or marginalize as mere "obliquities of presentation," the novel's rebarbative strategies of narrative disorientation, its sabotaging of conventional fictional expectations. But equally misleading are the reductive "modernist" versions of the text which shrivel its mimetic range and depth to a mere reflexive writhing, dismissing the massive, objective concretion of the social reality it deliberately constructs.

Neither perspective can accommodate the actual scope of a novel whose structure of meaning might best be described as a double spiral of simultaneous revelation *and* repression, critical exfoliation *and* legitimizing obfuscation. Driving through *Nostromo* is the compulsion to open up social-historical reality, to lay bare the concealed conjunction of corrupt motives and "material interests" producing a private and public history overtly condemned by Conrad as false and inhuman. But *at the same time* there is an equal counterthrust towards the opposite effect: the representation of reality as inherently unintelligible, as beyond objective cognition and moral evaluation. And the implicit ideological import of this counterperspective is clear. For instead of unmasking the prevailing social order as the all too explicable product of a changing human history, it tacitly underwrites and consolidates that order by ascribing to it the unfathomable, metaphysical status of an eternal human condition.

This tension between aperture and closure, cognitive penetration and blurring obstruction—writing as it were *sous rature*—is generated by the contradictory pressures under which Conrad narrates. Politically conservative, indeed reactionary as he is, when Conrad takes up his pen to work his fiction he enters a psychologically excruciating situation to which his anguished letters bear constant witness. For to fulfil the artistic pledge set forth in the Preface to *The Nigger of the "Narcissus,"* to make the reader see the truth of reality and thereby rouse him to that "subtle but invincible conviction of solidarity," leads Conrad necessarily to expose and indict the prevailing imperialist society which he otherwise endorses, and on whose validity, indeed, he stakes his social identity. "A single-minded attempt to render the highest kind of justice" to reality means an interrogation of the entire structure of presuppositions and values on which his ideological allegiance rests, an erosion of the very foundations of his subjectivity.

Writing is such an agony for Conrad because it involves this threat of psychological self-destruction, of reality and identity dissolving into "an unexplored universe of incertitudes." That striking phrase in *Lord Jim* where Marlow concedes that "enlightenment" had been brought into the

Archipelago "for the sake of better morality and—and—well—the greater profit too" graphically articulates the pressure under which Conrad forces out the truths which cut against the grain of the ruling consciousness to which he subscribes. But to transcend his divided self, to break completely with that false consciousness and emerge into a new, oppositional vision of reality, is beyond Conrad. Therefore he must contrive instead to write the truth of reality in such a way as to extinguish it *in the very moment* of its articulation. His narration must proceed in such a way as to engineer the coincident release and blockage of its otherwise insupportable revelations.

This, I think it could be argued, is the central dynamic of all Conrad's major fiction. We can see it most clearly at work if we turn for a moment to *Heart of Darkness*, whose title condenses in a phrase the cognitive tension between blindness and insight structuring this paradigmatic Conradian text. The narrative of Marlow—Conrad's recurrent means of internally distancing and so controlling his potentially self-destructive conflict as a writer—penetrates to the rotten heart of contemporary imperialist "civilisation," exposing and explaining its inhuman essence; and in the same breath it floods that recognition in metaphysical darkness, transforming the knowable heart of this historically produced reality into an enigmatic, impenetrable void. This deadlocking strategy of revelation and repression organizes the text from beginning to end.

Thus on the one hand the narrative cuts clean through all the lies and cosmetic rhetoric—through the ideology—to lay bare the rapacious and murderous barbarity of colonialism in Africa. The Company's office is recognized at once as "a house in the city of the dead" whose door is the door to hell. From the beginning, having intimated to his enthusing aunt that "the Company was run for profit" not philanthropy, Marlow feels himself "an imposter" alienated from his own humanity, contaminated by the moral fraudulence of the whole enterprise. When he arrives at the Company's station he denounces it as run by the "flabby, pretending, weak-eyed devil of a rapacious folly" and discerns its achievements all too clearly in the infernal grove of dying blacks reduced to mere "bundles of acute angles." The colonialist exploiters and parasites, the sarcastically dubbed "pilgrims," are excoriated throughout as the predatory walking dead, the *papier-mâché* hollow men with "nothing inside but a little loose dirt."

Nor, even before Marlow reaches Kurtz, is there any doubt as to the sordid rationale of "the horror." Kurtz "had collected, bartered, swindled, or stolen more ivory than all the other agents together" and "evidently the appetite for more ivory had got the better of the—what shall I say?—less material aspirations." And, when at last reached, Kurtz is identified as the dreadful epitome of the dehumanization and reification (he seems "carved out of old ivory," his very skull an "ivory ball") at the heart of an all-devouring imperialism: "I saw him open his mouth wide—it gave him a weirdly voracious aspect, as though he had wanted to swallow all the air, all the earth, all the men before him." This ruthless drive to strip all pretence away climaxes in Marlow's recognition that with his decision to remain "loyal" to Kurtz, to tell the lie and so preserve the ruling false consciousness, he himself is now "numbered with the dead." For he thereby conspires in concealing the very imperialist barbarity he has indicted throughout and thus sustains the smug citizens of the "sepulchral city," who blindly feed off the inhuman horror deliberately perpetrated on their behalf.

But although he exposes the lie *as* a lie, Conrad must simultaneously legitimize that lie as the only way to maintain "that great and saving illusion," to destroy which "would have been too dark—too dark altogether." The lie is thus a paradigm of the self-cancelling strategy central to the whole novel. For in the face of its own clear-sighted articulation of the social nature and cause of "the horror," the text insists on the irredeemably cryptic nature of the reality Marlow experiences, rewriting "the horror" as the inherent quality of a now metaphysically conceived "human condition" of meaningless futility, implicitly beyond man's choice and control. Within this perspective the novel simultaneously reworks Marlow's objective experience of colonial actuality, transmuting it into a mystical *voyage intérieur* "within the toil of a mournful and senseless delusion." The brutal exploitation is dehistoricized and desubstantialized, reconstrued now as a nightmarish phantom world, as "an unfathomable enigma" defying cognition by the density of its darkness or its blinding whiteness, by its absolute emptiness and utter, inscrutable silence. The deliberate dissection of the heart of imperialism can only proceed, so to speak, under the anaesthetic mystification of life as "that mysterious arrangement of merciless logic for a futile purpose."

The same splicing of critique and legitimation, the drive to display the true historical construction of the changing world inextricably crosswoven with the counterdrive to *ontologize* the historical in the service of the status quo, determines the form and meaning of *Nostromo*. For, in relating the history of the founding of the Sulacan Republic as a modern capitalist state within the controlling matrix of American imperialism, Conrad again inflicts on himself the narrative exploration of a social order he instinctively endorses, but whose unjust, dehumanizing rationale and alienating consequences he apprehends with painful clarity.

Indeed the creative anguish, the mind-snapping tension between the subversive unmasking and the occlusive confirmation of the prevailing social order, is more acute than ever with *Nostromo*, "the most anxiously meditated of [my] longer novels." The razor's edge sense of his dilemma is conveyed with nightmare precision in a letter of 1903 to Wells soon after beginning the novel: "I . . . am absolutely out of my mind with the worry and apprehension of my work. I go as one would cycle over a precipice along a 14-inch plank. If I falter I am lost." It is also, significantly, the closing stages of the ordeal of *Nostromo* that generate Conrad's trenchant definition of himself as "a *homo duplex*, in more than one sense." For in *Nostromo* Conrad must once again both clearly see and yet be blind to "the visible universe," ever disclosing yet veiling the actual composition and movement of reality in a truly "duplex" tension whereby the novel is at once propelled and paralyzed.

Thus on the one hand, in order to penetrate the ideological facade concealing the full historical and human truth, *Nostromo* deploys a range of strategies designed to deconstruct the bourgeois version of history and the whole "adventure novel" genre tendentially disposed to embody it. The text ruthlessly subverts all expectations of the kind of realist novel of epic action and exotic escapade which the title, subtitle and opening chapter deceptively arouse. In so doing it embodies an aggressive refusal of the hegemonic "providential" conception of history which finds ready mediation in the heroic and "colourful" historical "yarn." That conception is, indeed, ironically salienced within the novel in the pompous, complacent discourse of Captain Mitchell. And in a sense the whole novel can be understood as a dislocation and fracturing of the Captain Mitchell version of Sulaco's history: a labyrinthine excavation of the truth buried beneath the glib public lie distilled in Mitchell's "stereotyped relation of the 'historical events,'" his mythologized official account of how Sulaco became the "Treasure House of the World."

What *Nostromo* refuses to deliver is an orthodox, chronologically coherent narrative which, by culminating in a climactic struggle for and founding of the Sulacan Republic, would implicitly consecrate that culmination as the realized "aim" of a dovetailing historical process: the legitimizing point at which all the particular and general human fates would converge and find their purposive rationale, their retrospective *sense*. This whole structure of thinking, with its tacit teleological assumption of the modern capitalist state within imperialism as the natural "end" of history, is exploded by *Nostromo*'s violations of conventional narrative expectations.

Thus what would otherwise be the epic historical consummation of the fight for Sulaco is defused at once, robbed of its sense and teleological impact as Mitchell's "memorable occasion" by being prematurely broached and stranded right at the opening in chapter 2. This anticlimactic effect is multiplied throughout by similar deconstructive prolepses, most notably in part 3, when the action builds towards a momentous climax in chapter 9—will Nostromo make the impossible ride to Cayta and save Sulaco?—and the next chapter brusquely deflates that expectation, along with its sense of an imminent historical ending, by refusing to relate Nostromo's "famous ride to Cayta" and instead displacing the entire account of the winning of Sulaco into the stale retrospective of Mitchell. "The history of that ride, sir," says the Captain in a resonantly ironic remark, "would make a most exciting book." Indeed: precisely the kind of book Conrad's integrity cannot permit *Nostromo* to be.

This puncturing elision of the heroic ride foregrounds another crucial deconstructive strategy: the contradictory tension between the title and the actual *absence* of Nostromo from the centre of the "historical" action. The recurrent myth, vital to the Mitchellesque strand within bourgeois ideology, is that of history being made by the colourful Garibaldian "Man of the People"—a myth calculated to conceal the ruling economic and class interests actually constructing history. A monument to the Separation, says Mitchell, "could not do better than begin with the name of Nostromo," and that of course is exactly what Conrad's novel does *begin* with. But, having seen and understood that history is in fact made in the "material interests" and at the discretion of the Goulds, the Sir Johns and the Holroyds, Conrad can no longer write as if it were made by the Nostromos—by "our man" on behalf of all of us. And Conrad articulates this recognition, that Nostromo cannot be "the hero of the Tale of the Seaboard" because in reality "silver is the pivot of the moral and material events," by writing a novel whose putative hero can never become its hero, a novel which stubbornly refuses to acknowledge its own protagonist.

This demythologizing of the "illustrious Capataz de Cargadores," of the Nostromo flagrantly indulged for a moment in that "exotic" scene with the Morenita, proceeds through his conspicuous relegation to the periphery of his own story. The whole of part 1 and most of part 2 are haunted by a Nostromo glimpsed repeatedly on the margins, in the mere interstices of the main narrative concerns. In his fleeting appearance at the endangered Casa Viola or as Sir John's escort—"a most useful fellow"—at the edge of the firelight; as the "phantom-like horseman" materializing to solve the Company's labour problems or passing mysteriously beneath Antonia and Decoud on Gould's balcony, Nostromo always seems *about to* endorse the novel's title and snatch up the reins of the narrative. But he remains doomed to its verges by Conrad's uncompromising recognition of his real objective status as a blind tool of the ruling classes. And when Nostromo does at last move to the seeming centre in the Placido Gulf sequence it is only to discover that his "legendary" act of saving the silver is in fact of no vital consequence and that he himself is thoroughly dispensable. Likewise his momentous ride to Cayta cannot be represented as a climactic feat of unalloyed heroism because, as Conrad brings Nostromo himself to see, his daring courage served but to save "the lives and fortunes of the Blancos, the taskmasters of the people." His heroism is polluted by its complicity in securing the continuance of an oppressive social order, whose historical course is actually dictated by the propertied minority. Hence, insofar as his own personal tragedy as slave of the silver is allowed at last to occupy the close of the novel, it is as the mere postscript to a history callously indifferent to him.

The same demythologizing drive, moreover, powers Conrad's tunnelling beneath the facades of all the major characters. Narrative progression is repeatedly surrendered to extended retrospective probings beneath the mythical official selves preserved in Mitchell's pantheon and encoded in the characters' recurrent epithets (the vestiges, so to speak, of the identities they would have preserved unchallenged in the "straight" adventure novel Conrad could not write.) Thus Conrad peels back the public versions of the Goulds—"El Rey" and "the First Lady" of Sulaco—to reveal a man spiritually congealed and utterly alienated from his wife, "alone within a circumvallation of precious metal"; and a woman, the universally revered "Doña Emilia," disillusioned, lonely and guilt-ridden, "in the grip of a merciless nightmare" from which she cannot awake. In the Goulds Conrad exposes the self-deluding hollowness of the liberal rhetoric of progress and philanthropy legitimizing private enterprise: the soul-destroying contradiction between the cosmetic ideology and the dehumanizing reality of exploitation and corruption it conceals. And of course the pressure to demythologize exerts itself no less on the historically superseded figures of Don José Avellanos and "the heroic Giorgio Viola," as also on the romantic Mitchellesque version of Decoud, "the brilliant Costaguanero of the boulevards," who in fact ends as the mere alienated ghost of himself, literally sinking in despair beneath the weight of the all-powerful silver, the capital which, as Conrad intimated, is the real protagonist of this inhuman history.

This irrepressible compulsion to tear the ideological veil from historical reality issues towards the end in increasingly explicit, apodictic statements of the truths the text cannot evade. Thus the disabused Nostromo discovers through his own experience that "Kings, ministers, aristocrats, the rich in general, kept the people in poverty and subjection; they kept them as they kept dogs, to fight and hunt for their service." Monygham pronounces his devastating critique and prophecy:

> "There is no peace and no rest in the development of material interests. They have their law and their justice. But it is founded on expediency, and is inhuman . . . Mrs Gould, the time approaches when all that the Gould Concession stands for shall weigh as heavily upon the people as the barbarism, cruelty and misrule of a few years back."

And as for Mrs Gould herself:

> "She saw the San Tomé mountain hanging over the Campo, over the whole land, feared, hated, wealthy; more soulless than any tyrant, more pitiless and aristocratic than the worst government, ready to crush innumerable lives in the expansion of its greatness."

Given this order of recognition, moreover, the novel is further able to glimpse the emergence of those oppositional forces destined to challenge the whole social structure of which the mine is a function. Mitchell himself is alert to "these socialistic Italians" now drawing even the natives towards their new Democratic party; and, "by a stroke of astonishing intuition," as Arnold Kettle observes, alone at Nostromo's deathbed is placed the Communist, at whom Conrad has the "Man of the People" direct "a glance of enigmatic and profound enquiry." In short, the whole deconstructive trajectory of *Nostromo* embodies a genuinely *historicizing* dynamic, illuminating the real formation and motion of society in history—history being grasped as a humanly produced, changing and changeable process whose rationale, laws and consequences are not only fully intelligible but susceptible of definite moral evaluation.

But this historicizing impulse is simultaneously cancelled by the pervasive ontologizing pressure exerted within and across the deconstructed sectors of the text by *Nostromo's* basic *descriptive* style. What is opened up on one plane as intelligibly developing history made by men is written out on another intersecting plane as an opaque, unchanging condition devoid of meaning and beyond evaluation. That his fundamental style of writing serves a deep need to evade or repress forbidden dimensions of cognition is suggested by Conrad himself in a striking remark whose full measure we can now begin to take: "It is evident that my fate is to be descriptive and descriptive only. There are things I *must* leave alone." Exactly how "description" supplies Conrad with the means of forestalling, blocking or neutralizing his own sure critical penetration of historical reality becomes clear if we look at Lukács's critique of the "naturalistic" style in his classic essay "Narrate or Describe?"

Focusing on Zola and Flaubert (Conrad's acknowledged master, of course), Lukács shows how the reductive and deforming "descriptive" method is produced by, and itself reflects, the intensely alienated experience of life in the imperialist era, "the domination of capitalist prose over the inner poetry of human experience, the continuous dehumanization of social life, the general debasement of humanity." For in its painfully honest endeavour to mirror reality "as it really is," with scrupulously detailed, comprehensive objectivity, naturalistic writing in fact ends up with an essentially static, two-dimensional, surface *description* of its subject instead of a dynamic, three-dimensional and processive *narration* of it grasped both from within and without. The descriptive approach hypostatizes the current imperialist order, investing its degrading but transient reality with an absolute and universal status. It robs human life of all sense of being made out of the transformative interaction of men and women with each other and with their natural and social world.

The descriptive strategy of *Nostromo* is most immediately evident in its meandering mode of advance through set-piece tableaux rendered with a lingering profusion of detailed circumstance. One thinks of the opening friezes of life at the Casa Viola; of the O.S.N. *convité* on the *Juno*; of the Goulds frozen silent in their house; the troops' embarkation under Barrios; the Goulds' party, with Decoud and Antonia on the balcony; Decoud alone at night in the Casa Viola; the hypnotic Placido Gulf scene; Nostromo and Monygham spellbound before the grotesque suspended corpse of Hirsch; Decoud lost out of time in the infinite solitude of the island. The novel delivers no sense of developing action emerging through the vital interplay of the characters with each other and their world. Quite the reverse. The narration does not flow, it coils and eddies through a configuration of still centres, congealed *settings for* action which, if recounted at all, is not fully narrated from the "inside" as well—through the evolving subjectivity of active participants—but statically depicted as a ready-made phenomenon, a finished product. The essential "action" of *Nostromo* is treated as something that, in an absolute sense, *has already happened*, that was, as it were, over and sealed off before the author arrived; not as a *process* to be represented in its full dialectical composition and movement.

Instead of writer and reader actively collaborating in the exploration of an unfolding human experience, both are reduced by description to passive observers of a dead world, fixed and frozen in advance. The characters in *Nostromo* are presented either as given and fixed thus or, insofar as they exhibit change, as subsequently *having become* thus: they are presented, in other words, as *results*. There transpires no inwardly illuminated, conflictive drama of becoming, for "description provides no true poetry of things but transforms people into conditions, into components of still lives . . . The result is a series of static pictures . . . The so-called action is only a thread on which the still lives are disposed in a superficial, ineffective, fortuitous sequence of isolated, static pictures."

In *Nostromo* there is no real *exchange* either of language or experience. The pervasive sense of stasis, of almost lifeless reification, is immediately evident in the descriptions of the characters. Giorgio's face has "the immobility of a carving" and to the end he remains "unstirring, like a statue of an old man." The Sulaco ladies "looked like white plaster casts with beautiful living eyes." Mrs. Gould, "her face powdered white like a plaster cast," confronts a people "suffering and mute, waiting for the future in a pathetic immobility of patience." She is repeatedly depicted in withdrawn poses, and the conclusion leaves her frozen in "her still and sad immobility," displaying "the charm of an attitude caught and interpreted for ever." Nostromo likewise appears typically waiting, "silent on a motionless horse" or transfixed in "silence and immobility." Don José "appeared almost inanimate, sitting rigidly by the side of Mrs Gould," his face "as if modelled in yellow wax." Father Corbelán "remained quite motionless . . . with that something vengeful in his immobility." Pedrito Montero "became motionless and silent as if turned into stone." The characters' state of paralysis and petrifaction is intensified throughout, moreover, by the quality of the surrounding world: "outside the house there was a great silence"; everything is "steeped in a clear stillness as in an imponderable liquid."

This vision of an inherently dehumanized world of stone and statue, reified beyond all hope of human transformation, finds condensed symbolic expression in various haunting focal images: the mountain Higuerota, periodically looming forth over Sulaco "like a frozen bubble under the moon"; the enigmatic corpse of Hirsch, "suspended in his awful immobility"; above all the image of Decoud and Nostromo motionless in the viscous blackness of the Placido Gulf. For there the occlusive, metaphysical countervision of the novel finds its supreme imaginative realization in an apocalyptic anti-climax of absolute stillness, silence, emptiness and deathlike darkness. Reality dissolves within "the thick veil of obscurity that felt warm and hopeless all about them." It is one of Conrad's most compelling sustained images of nihilistic despair in the face of an utterly illusory and unknowable reality: "No intelligence could penetrate the darkness of the Placid Gulf."

This dehistoricizing, coagulative impulse crystallizes out in authorial pronouncements in direct conflict with the trenchant critical recognitions articulated through Nostromo, Mrs Gould and Monygham. Thus, although the text reveals only too clearly why the Sulacan people suffer, and will continue to suffer, under the *"imperium in imperio"* of Gould and the whole social order he represents, Conrad can nevertheless conclude from the scene in which Gould observes a woman kneeling by the side of a dying *cargador*, mortally wounded while defending the interests of the mine: "The cruel futility of things stood unveiled in the levity and sufferings of that incorrigible people; the cruel futility of lives and deaths thrown away in the vain endeavour to attain an enduring solution of the problem." This metaphysical blurring climaxes in the categorical generalizations proliferating around Decoud's suicide: "In our activity alone do we find the sustaining illusion of an independent existence as against the whole scheme of things of which we form a helpless part." Decoud disappears "without trace, swallowed up in the immense indifference of things."

Nostromo's convergence of critical revelation and mystifying closure has the effect of a continuous suppressed explosion. Within the deconstructive perspective the dispersive drive of the narrative forces the reader to respond in an intensely critical way—analysing, discriminating, inferring and synthesizing, reconstructing an authentic, oppositional version of the private and public history of Sulaco. In this sense *Nostromo* indeed "succeeds most wonderfully in capturing the truth of social movement," its achievement being "nothing less than the presentation . . . of society in motion, history in the making." But the dispersed, tesselated sectors of *Nostromo* are concurrently subdued to a stylistic pressure which thickens and reifies the deconstructively disclosed world, which freezes character and paralyzes action, ontologizing and thus evacuating the historical, which nevertheless survives as a pervasive, insistent *absence* swelling beneath the surface of the text. It is this dimension of the novel which accounts for Leavis's troubled intuition that "for all the rich variety of the interest and the tightness of the pattern, the reverberation of *Nostromo* has something hollow about it; with the colour and life there is a suggestion of a certain emptiness." It is what accounts, in short, for that sense one has with Conrad that "in working his fiction . . . the writer is shaping a vacuum, sculpting a void." [Terry Eagleton, *Criticism and Ideology*].

"So foul a sky clears not without a storm": as the novel's epigraph confirms in its presiding image of congestion and explosive tension, the central structure of feeling organizing *Nostromo* is that of radical impasse, of deadlocking self-cancellation. It's surely just this profound sense of blockage stemming the clear flow through of the fictive vision that explains Conrad's own intriguing judgment of the novel in a letter to Gide in 1912: "But it doesn't work; that is true. There is something that prevents it from working. I don't know what. All in all, even with all my tenderness, I myself cannot stand to read it." Conrad is here circling once again round the cryptic heart of his own productive impulse. In grasping *Nostromo*'s constitutive double dynamic of revelation and repression we can, I think, move closer to a full understanding of the nature of that impulse and thus a clearer comprehension of the quality and value of his fiction as a whole.

Nostromo: Conrad's Organicist Philosophy of History

T. McAlindon

At the beginning of "Youth," Conrad sets up an ironic antithesis between Frederick Burnaby's *Ride to Khiva* and Carlyle's *Sartor Resartus*. The former, a popular piece of Victorian travel literature instinct with "the absolutely pure, uncalculating, unpractical spirit of adventure," is admired by Marlow. The latter, an idiosyncratic expression of representative nineteenth-century ideas about man and history, is disliked by Marlow and poorly comprehended.

Each book could be described as an odyssey. *Sartor Resartus*, however, is a spiritual odyssey, and one in which its hero, Teufelsdröckh, progresses toward a mature vision of reality. Acquiring his so-called "clothes philosophy," he learns to pierce the vesture of things and to discriminate between authentic and false values. He becomes convinced that the greatest evils in life are "dilettantism" (skepticism, an incapacity for wonder and worship), "dandyism" (self-worship) and sham (an adherence to outmoded and irrelevant forms of belief). These evils pervert man's instinct for obedience, reverence and hero-worship, an instinct which has been the cornerstone of religion and society at all times. Teufelsdröckh's interest in hero-worship leads him thus to consider man's nature and destiny from a grand historical perspective where the blinding effects of space and time (more false appearance) are transcended. He perceives that great men are the divine in human form and that as such they establish an organic unity not only among the living but among all men at all times. They are the clearest proof that the world is really a "spectral Necropolis, or rather City both of the Dead and of the Unborn, where the Present seems little other than an inconsiderable

From *Mosaic* 15, no. 3 (September 1982). © 1982 by Mosaic.

Film dividing the Past and the Future." Teufelsdröckh comes to rest therefore on an "organicist" philosophy of history which incorporates a philosophy of religion and of heroism.

To return with all this in mind to "Youth" and its companion piece *Heart of Darkness* is to perceive instantly the irony implicit in Marlow's offhand treatment of *Sartor Resartus*. For in these two tales Marlow is required to discriminate between authentic and false heroism. He comes to reflect more and more on the momentous implications of work, duty and faith, of hero-worship and idolatry. His experiences, too, are subtly removed from ordinariness by their religious coloring and by their relation to analogous events in widely different phases of history. In fact so spacious is the religio-historical perspective that the reader is brought face to face with what Carlyle calls "universal history" and what Conrad—in thoroughly Carlylean terms—calls "truth stripped of its cloak of time."

The effects on *Lord Jim* of the ideas which Carlyle had stereotyped are hardly less obvious. But as I hope to illustrate, it is in *Nostromo* that their impact on Conrad's thought and art shows most profoundly.

Nostromo, of course, is a novel obsessed with history. Indeed most of its characters can be divided into those who consciously turn their backs on the past (Holroyd, Sir John, Charles Gould) and those who frequently and in some cases continually reflect on it. Those in the second group are in the majority, and on the whole their common bias commands our respect or at least our sympathy. It is clear, however, that historical consciousness does not necessarily involve historical understanding. This applies even to the narrator, whose voice is often that of the author but who frequently reminisces in a benign or panegyric manner discrepant with the drift of the historical material itself. Continually, the reader is forced to question his authorities, sift the evidence, and draw his own conclusions—of which the most important is that the past goes on repeating itself. The total history as well as the individual biographies of which it is composed evince a cyclical pattern. This pattern is underlined by means of suggestive imagery and wordplay, and indirectly reinforced by the time-shift technique which, by arbitrarily interchanging future, past and present, undermines the linear-progressive view of history.

There is undoubtedly much to suggest that the novel's historical philosophy is rigidly determinist and pessimistic. Decoud's horrified fear of "finding himself in the water and swimming, overwhelmed by ignorance and darkness, probably in a circle, till he sank from exhaustion," may be invalidated as an intuition of the true nature of things by the narrator's severe moral strictures on Decoud's lack of faith. But it is upheld by the nature of that political future for which the editor of *The Future* (*El Porvenir*) worked so hard, since his independent state will soon slip back into the federalism from which he has helped to rescue it. Moreover, Decoud has earlier spelled out the notion of futile, historical circularity with a cold percipience which seems to suggest that his voice is at that point the voice of Conrad. Hearing the explosive noise of the railway engine, he reflects that the Anglo-Saxons of today are about to do what the adventurous Drake and his buccaneers did to his Spanish forefathers: "It has always been the same."

Yet for all his sense of historical irony, Decoud's view of the relationship between past and present is still a shortsighted one. To go beyond Don José's fifty-year perspective on Costaguana's present troubles is commendable; but it is a great error to assume that the violent process of robbery and exploitation began with those adventurers who sought to dispossess his quixotic ancestors. Thus we are also told in this same passage that the engine entering Sulaco emitted a "prolonged scream of warlike triumph" which startled the silent people (returning from a *military* spectacle) and finally stopped with "the clanking of chain couplings" and "a tumult of blows and shaken fetters." Throughout the novel there are many such images of the Indians numbed by centuries of poverty and domination, "waiting for the future with a pathetic immobility of patience." Nothing has changed for them since Decoud's "wonderful people" arrived on their shores to turn them into Christians and slaves.

With the exception of Monygham, who finds in "the dark passages of . . . history" a salutary reminder of personal weakness, everyone in Costaguana who turns to the past does so in the interest of his own "exalted egoism." Emilia undoubtedly "knew the history of the San Tomé mine" and therefore knew that "whole tribes of Indians perished in the exploitation"; but this historical fact does not impinge upon her conception of the great adventure on which she and her husband are embarked. It is only when the disillusion of a wasted lifetime descends upon her that she comes near to an understanding of the whole endeavor. Half-consciously, and in purely personal terms, she formulates the novel's guiding norm on the conditions of life in time: "It had come into her mind that for life to be large and full, it must contain the care of the past and of the future in every passing moment of the present. Our daily work must be done to the glory of the dead, and for the good of those who come after."

It would seem then that self-knowledge of the historical kind offers an escape from the tragic circle. But whether mankind in general, or its leaders in particular, are capable of such knowledge is left an open question at the end. For not only is the final picture unpromising; the novel has, in addition to its cyclical patterns, a fine network of historical analogies and echoes which seem designed to prove that the connections between past, present and future consist of "organic filaments" (Carlyle's terminology) which are certain to elude the unvigilant eye. History may be, as Teufelsdröckh discovered, "a perpetual evangel," but its print, like that of old Giorgio's Bible, is extremely small.

The reader of *Nostromo*, however, is invited to become a speculative Romantic historian and to search among the disregarded fragments of time for an eloquent omnitemporal coherence. To respond to this invitation may well be to incur on occasion the charge of mere ingenuity; but enough of substance should emerge to establish that an organic theory of history informs the structure and texture of the novel, and to establish too that this theory embraces a theory of heroism and religion.

Incorporate and partly obvious in the design of *Nostromo* is the pattern of Spanish imperial history in the fifteenth and sixteenth centuries. This incorporation is effected not just by means of archaeological detail and periodic reference to the *Conquistadores*. As we shall see, Conrad's method of characterization and his cunning use of names and other associative devices are such that the great individuals of the past seem reincarnate in the *dramatis personae* of the present. It may be, however, that for the educated reader of 1904 the most immediately effective method of relating present to past in *Nostromo* was Conrad's application to contemporary events of the ideas which dominate the authoritative nineteenth-century account of the Spanish Conquest and its political background — W. H. Prescott's *The Reign of Ferdinand and Isabella, The Conquest of Mexico* and *The Conquest of Peru*. Conrad exploits not only the Conquest and the Conquerors but the meanings conferred upon them by one of the most respected and widely read of nineteenth-century liberal historians.

Perhaps the most conspicuous theme in Prescott is the almost incomprehensible confusion of the material and the spiritual in the motives of the Spaniards. At home and abroad, they are shown to have been fanatical inquisitors and missionaries who were just as sincere in their desire to impose "pure and uncorrupted doctrine" on heretics, infidels and heathens as they were to appropriate their wealth. Prescott is lavishly deferential to the spirit of romantic adventure which actuated the Conquerors and habitually represents them as literal embodiments of that extravagant knight-errantry which is part of the Spanish myth. But he is conscious, too, of the sinister frivolity inherent in political adventurism and repeatedly refers to it as a game in which great men participated like desperate gamblers irrespective of the cost in human life.

So prominent are these themes and metaphors in *Nostromo* that exemplification is unnecessary. But one parallel deserves detailed attention since it is sufficiently striking to preclude the possibility that the resemblances are coincidental, and since, moreover, it involves the final verdict of each author on the heroic endeavors of his principal characters. Despite his intense admiration for the founders of the Spanish Empire, and especially for the great Isabella and for Columbus, Prescott brings his account of the reign of Ferdinand and Isabella to a conclusion with some melancholy reflections which serve to invalidate the whole imperial adventure. Since, he remarks, "the discovery of a world was estimated, like that of a mine, by the value of its returns in gold and silver," the colonies soon became "miserably dwarfed in their growth" and the mother country itself was eventually impoverished by its very wealth:

> *The streams of wealth which flowed in from the silver quarries* of Zacatecas and Potosi were jealously locked up within the limits of the Peninsula. The great problem proposed by the Spanish legislation of the sixteenth century was the reduction of prices in the kingdom to the same level as in other European nations. Every law that was passed, however, tended, by its restrictive character, to augment the evil. *The golden tide, which, permitted a free vent, would have fertilized the region through which it poured, now buried the land under a deluge which blighted every green and living thing.* Agriculture, commerce, manufactures, every branch of national industry and improvement, languished and fell to decay; and the nation, *like the Phrygian monarch who turned all that he touched to gold, was poor in the midst of its treasures* [emphasis mine].
>
> (*The Reign of Ferdinand and Isabella*)

This summary judgment is echoed in Conrad's conception of the tragic success of Charles and Emilia Gould. The great "stream of silver" which flows down from San Tomé—this is a recurrent metaphor—literally blights the green mountain before it is jealously locked up in the Custom House and shipped off to San Francisco. Moreover, this triumph over nature leaves Charles Gould (Gold?) dwelling Midas-like "within a circumvallation of precious metal" and his wife "all alone in the Treasure House of the World," conscious only of the degradation of their young ideal.

Since "The Treasure House of the World" was the name given by Sir Francis Drake to the Indies, and since the motives of the Goulds and their patron contain ideas of conquest, one can be reasonably certain that Conrad sees in the history of Charles and Emilia the recurrence of an old catastrophe. There is even a strong resemblance between the contrasting personalities and the blighted relationship of Charles and Emilia, on the one hand,

and of Ferdinand and Isabella, on the other; but it is perhaps better to leave this as another one of the many tantalizing possibilities with which the novel deliberately (I believe) confronts us. There can, however, be little doubt that in the name and history of the novel's titular hero, and in the name of the island where he meets his doom, Conrad seeks to provide a recurrent echo of Columbus and of the great queen whose enlightened patronage gave him his glory and Spain its empire.

Columbus, it will be remembered, was a proud man of humble origin who died convinced that he was exploited and betrayed by a cold, sagacious king. So too is Nostromo. Columbus was brought back in chains from the Indies and died in poverty, commanding that "the ignominious fetters" (as Prescott calls them) be hung above his bed. So too when the willing instrument of "the King of Sulaco" goes to meet his death on the Great Isabel, all he can hear in the silence of the night is the clanking of his own "shameful fetters." Columbus moreover was a Genoese sailor, and so is Nostromo: indeed he is frequently referred to in no other way. The most suggestive instances of this trick occur in the course of Decoud's ironically imperceptive monologue on the achievements and misfortunes of his Spanish ancestors: "That is history . . . that's really the work of that Genoese seaman!"

The radical confusion of motive which afflicts the adventurers and conquerors of Costaguana is what relates them most positively to their historical and legendary predecessors. And as in their predecessors, the principal sign of this confusion lies in their religious outlook. The religious element in *Nostromo* has, however, an importance which cannot be ascribed simply to its role as a source of historical analogy; it involves the central concerns of the novel and does so in such a way as to corroborate Carlyle's claim that the principal key to history lies in what men believe and worship, in their religion or no-religion.

Religion enters the novel on both the figurative and the literal planes. Not only are there numerous references to religious beliefs, practices and objects; the style is everywhere informed with religious and mythological metaphor. Indeed so colored is the language by the idea of religion that a specifically religious stylistic mode—the iconographic, as I shall call it—is evolved. An invariable symptom of this style is the use of the word "immobile" or "motionless." Of course this is one of the most characteristic epithets in Conrad's fiction as a whole, a fact we may ascribe to his preoccupation with states of spiritual paralysis and to his belief that fiction should aspire to the plasticity of sculpture and the color of painting. Although such explanations are broadly relevant to *Nostromo*, this novel's insistent representation of the individual in statuesque poses is functionally related to its own controlling ideas about religion-and-history.

In general the iconographic style in *Nostromo* creates the impression that the world itself is a great temple or shrine filled with images of divinities and saints and their throng of ardent worshippers; it conspires thus with characterization and plot to suggest that all human bonds are essentially bonds of faith between the worshipped and the worshipper, protector and protegé. More particularly, the iconographic style establishes a perspective from which we see that the living and the dying are already in the process of being absorbed by history, and that the paradigms of myth, religion and history are all one. Consider, for example, the extended description of "the old Garibaldino" seated with "the immobility of a carving" beneath "the coloured lithograph of Garibaldi" and reflecting that "the man was a saint," an "immortal hero." This has to be remembered at the end of the novel when "the old Garibaldino," himself now designated as "the hero without stain," stands "rugged and unstirring" over the body of Nostromo "like a statue of an old man guarding the honour of his house." But the colored lithograph of Garibaldi, with its motionless worshipper, must also be recalled when the most fanatical of Nostromo's admirers, the little photographer, is pictured beside the bed where his hero dies "without a word or moan after an hour of immobility."

On the other hand, the iconographic style insidiously suggests (in passages like these) that the heroes and saints had serious defects which are concealed by the flattering arts of sculptor, lithographer and photographer. Furthermore, it exposes the deadly, dual process of treating human beings as objects and of investing material objects with spiritual worth. Because of Gould's facility for dressing his silver in "the fair robes of an idea," Emilia becomes no more real to him than the blue-robed Madonna in their ancestral Spanish home; and Charles himself, forever mounted on his "slate-coloured beast," becomes as cold and inscrutable as the equestrian statue of his predecessor Charles IV, the last king to rule over South America.

More conspicuous than these motives in the religious argument is the missionary act of replacing a native mythology with a foreign one. Conrad is concerned to expose the unnaturalness and the sham quality of colonial evangelizing, and he does so in his most oblique and tactful manner. Thus he establishes in chapters 1 and 2 an implicit antithesis between the quiet, unknown gods who hitherto have found an inviolate sanctuary under the snowy dome of Higuerota, and the gods of Olympus, whose names are resolutely introduced to the tame Indians by the little black steamers of the O.S.N. Company. The dangerously confused and deceptive character of this new mythology is pinpointed with a nice blend of pun, paradox and metaphor in the passage telling how Gould's guests left Sulaco on board the *Ceres,* which "was to carry them off into the Olympus of plutocrats." One recalls that the rape of Ceres by Pluto, god of Hell, blighted an earthly paradise. This opening shaft is remembered at the very end when it is recorded that the Occidental Republic faces the future with a New Custom House which has "the sham air of a Greek temple." New good customs are bad old ones in fancy dress.

But this is to speak only of the republic's unofficial imported religion, plutolatry. The official import is best approached through the complex figure of Father Corbelán, a priest whose social and political outlook give him a deceptively progressivist air. Corbelán's obsession with restoring to the Church all the material signs of its spiritual ascendancy connects him with the time between Charles IV and the Great Isabel, when everything was for the padres and nothing for the people. Yet there is something heroic in his life-style which recalls the ideal past of the hagiographers. An indefatigable "converter of savage Indians," he displays so much "apostolic zeal" that he is revered by the faithful as a miracle worker and a living saint. Indeed his legendary feat of baptizing single-handed "whole nations of Indians" identifies him with two missionary saints who are known in the Catholic calendar as the patrons of India—the apostle Thomas himself, and St. Francis (Xavier). But to recognize this parallel is to come to strange conclusions about the role of Christianity in Costaguana. It is to perceive that the link between San Tomé and San Francisco—on which the welfare of everyone, and especially that of the so-called Indians, is thought to depend—constitutes one of Conrad's deepest ironies. Sanctuaries to which all look for protection and a ray of light, relics of a corrupted ideal, these two places are arguably the novel's most important symbols of historical betrayal and sham. Their ironic function, too, is greatly enhanced at the end when Cardinal Corbelán and "the heroic Father Román" gird themselves to resist the missionaries who are on their way from San Francisco with a yet purer form of religion for the benighted Indians.

The dark side of Corbelán's religion is most apparent in his fanatical intolerance of "heretics": the last of the Corbeláns is a figure from the Inquisition. The honor done to Sulaco by his elevation to the College of Cardinals at the end is singularly fitting, since the historic importance the place is said to have enjoyed "in the olden time" is ascribed to the fact that "the highest ecclesiastical court" had its seat there. At any rate, Corbelán's curious insistence on lodging in the ruins of an old Dominican convent whenever he returns from the wilds to Sulaco is an assertion of his historical identity, the Inquisition having been founded by one Domingo de Guzmán, better known as St. Dominic. There is the finest of filamental connections between the scar-faced Corbelán and that other "saintly bishop" whose broken-nosed statue, standing in the Amarilla Club, is mentioned from time to time. The name of this bishop is forgotten, but it is remembered that the historic quarters of the club were "once the residence of a high official of the Holy Office."

The perennial reality of the Inquisition, however, is much less palpable in Corbelán than in Father Berón and Guzman Bento. To the dictator, "Supreme Government had . . . become an object of strange worship, as if it were some cruel deity. It was incarnated in himself, and his adversaries, the Federalists, were the supreme sinners, objects of hate, abhorrence and fear, as heretics would be to a convinced Inquisitor." Father Berón is the archetypal priestly Inquisitor, serving still as an arm of the state; under Guzman Bento, "his inquisitorial instincts suffered but little from the want of classical apparatus of the Inquisition."

The novel's most important heretic is not Berón's twisted victim Doctor Monygham, but Charles Gould, the unrecanting materialist who to the end is "incorrigible in his devotion to the great silver mine." Emilia, of course, is the saint, madonna or divinity to whom he proves unfaithful; a near-perfect embodiment of human worth, she provokes in Monygham and others "ideas of adoration, of kissing the hem of her robe." Since all human bonds are conceived in *Nostromo* as bonds of faith between worshipped and worshipper, protector and protegé, the concepts of saint and divinity are generically equivalent. But they are also, on the whole, functionally distinguishable. The saint idea allows for emphasis on the personal and humane aspect of religion. Moreover, since the saint is the popular hero in religious guise, it provides a sociologically appropriate variation on the subject of heroism and its place in history. This variation recalls Carlyle, who refers to the hero as a "divine missionary" and a saint (albeit uncanonized) and claims that the heroes of history, the men of worth and worship (worth-ship), constitute "a living, literal *Communion of Saints* wide as the world itself, and as the history of the world."

Appropriately from the Carlylean point of view, the saint idea is located principally in Nostromo himself. To grasp the full implications of this fact, however, one must first perceive that a complementary idea in Carlyle's definition of the hero has gone into the creation of the Genoese seaman. This is the concept of the hero as King or Ableman, two titles which Carlyle treats as synonymous on the basis of a false etymology relating "king" to "can." Like Charles Gould, Nostromo is competence itself; and whereas in Gould's case this fact is expressed in the royal nickname, in Nostromo's it is insinuated by that grand title on which is played a number of resonant variations, of which the most cunning by far is "his worship the

Capataz." "Capataz" is the Spanish for foreman and is formed from the adjective "*capaz*," which, like the Latin "*capax*," means able or competent. Nostromo then is foreman, first man, and worshipped hero precisely because, like Tuan Jim, he is the personification of "Ability in the Abstract."

But more significant than Nostromo the Ableman is Nostromo the saint, the hero who is introduced in the first chapters as coming miraculously to the aid of socially unimportant but very ardent devotees. Menaced on all sides by the forces of darkness, Teresa Viola sits "muttering pious invocations to all the saints of the calendar." One saint however (to whom she "bent" her "knee" in the morning) dominates her prayers: " 'Oh! Gian' Battista, why art thou not here? Oh why art thou not here?' . . . She was not then invoking the saint himself, but calling upon Nostromo, whose patron he was." Whereas for Mitchell and the Company the Capataz is simply "our man," a marvellous tool, for Teresa and her daughters he is a remarkable human being who is loved as well as needed and admired. Thus they refuse to call him "Nostromo" and remind him and others that his real name is the one he was born with—Giovanni Battista Fidanza. This is a name which associates him with the first hero-saint of the Church, the first man to live and die for the faith. It establishes his moral identity and the conditions within which he can achieve authentic if unglamorous heroism. Thus the nature of Nostromo's tragedy is that he is not true to his name.

To be more precise, Gian' Battista's primary mission in life is to "save the children" and to fetch the priest who will save their—and his—mother's soul. Taking precedence over this, and claiming all his legendary abilities, is the mission to save the silver and the separatist movement. His success with the silver has the appearance of being, as he himself claims, "a miracle greater than any saint could perform"; and the success of his "famous ride to Cayta" is such that he will be remembered in history and on Parrochetti's monument as a hero without stain. But the truth is that his Worship the Capataz concludes as the mere vesture of a vanished worth and a dead faith: "everything was as before, only everything was a sham."

By a nice irony, therefore, Nostromo's end is similar to that of the unbelieving and anti-heroic Decoud. Although Decoud insists that he does not believe in miracles and that he has no mission in life, he does in fact undertake a mission and so goes down in history as "the young apostle of Separation" who "died striving for his idea by an ever-lamented accident." Since, however, he undertook the mission largely out of self-interest, and "died for want of faith in himself and others," he provides yet another sham hero for the reverend worship of posterity. "The apostle of Separation" is really a false honorific which quietly explains his radical incapacity for true heroism. As the author of *Sartor Resartus* remarked, "there is much, nay almost all in names"—they are the garment of the self.

Carlyle's ideas on the roles of belief, heroism and hero-worship in history have as much bearing on the character of Decoud as on that of Nostromo. But Decoud's skepticism is of far greater importance in this respect than is his final contribution to the worship of sham temples and sham heroes. Revering no one and nothing but himself and his own opinions, he is, as Corbelán suggests, the classic child of a faithless age: a "dilettante" who "dabbles" in literature and journalism, a "dandy" whose dress is silken, varnished, Frenchified. Obviously, he is modelled on the self-worshipping dandy and the skeptical dilettante of *Sartor Resartus*, those fiercely reviled and kindred human types who spurn hero-worship, "affect great purity and separatism," and "distinguish themselves by a particular costume." The manner of Decoud's death too recalls *Sartor Resartus*, his suicidal surrender to the blank vastness of the universe being a surrender to the Everlasting No, that terrible demon which drove Teufelsdröckh to the verge of suicide. The Everlasting No, explains Carlyle, induces "the fearful Unbelief . . . unbelief in yourself"; it makes one feel "a feeble unit in the middle of a threatening Infinitude."

It could be argued that the spurious or corrupt element in the heroism of all the politically important figures in *Nostromo* proves that Conrad's view of the hero and his place in history differs greatly from that of Carlyle. However, Carlyle does insist that a time of revolution is a time of disbelief when men either worship "the Sham-Hero" or disbelieve in the possibility of true greatness. Moreover he recognizes that great men—Napoleon is his chief example in this—can become in time the very antithesis of that truth and sincerity they once personified. It is true nevertheless that Conrad's constitutional skepticism—which is flagellated in the person of Decoud—affects his whole attitude to the heroic to the extent that *Nostromo* must be considered an imaginative critique as well as an exploration of the ideas which Carlyle had stereotyped. For Conrad's reservations about the hero seem to apply to the heroes of all time. He implies that those who dominate the history books and the public squares and shrines may not have been great at all in the true sense of the word, and that if they were great it was only in a very muddled or muddied fashion. He appears to believe that true human worth is always invisible to the majority and never affects the destiny of nations. Furthermore, although he shares Carlyle's attitude to faith and fidelity, the act of affirmation which leads to heroic involvement with others is not for him an Everlasting Yea based on some absolute truth. It proceeds more likely from a necessary fiction, a saving illusion.

Carlyle's insistence, however, on the cardinal function of heroism, worship and faith in the history of mankind must have been immensely useful to Conrad insofar as it encouraged him to approach the fiction of adventure and travel with a firm belief in its philosophic potential. More important, perhaps, the organic theory of history, stressing a vital and responsible relationship between past, present and future (a theory which we need not identify with Carlyle alone), prompted him to develop methods of narration in which a synoptic vision of human destiny, freed from the more obvious constrictions of time and space, is still compatible with naturalism and an acute sense of history. Strictly speaking, however (and *pace* Avrom Fleischman), *Nostromo* is not a historical novel, since instead of recreating the past and acknowledging its pastness it tends rather to establish that "Time present and time past / Are both perhaps present in time future / And time future contained in time past" (Eliot, "Burnt Norton"). In *The Rover* and *Suspense*, Conrad was to write historical fiction proper, but this is as different in kind from *Nostromo* as it is in quality; and the difference in quality may be due in large measure to the fact that of its very nature it did not require the great imaginative effort of imposing organic unity on the temporally and spatially discrete.

This effort has an important bearing on Conrad's position in the history of twentieth-century literature. In 1923, Eliot praised Joyce for perfecting a method of "controlling . . . ordering . . . giving a shape and a significance to the immense panorama of futility and anarchy which is contemporary history"; the method, he explained, was one of "manipulating a continuous parallel between contemporaneity and antiquity." Although Eliot adds that "the method was adumbrated by Mr. Yeats," he makes no mention of the dying Joseph Conrad. Which is very strange indeed. But whether they would have given him credit for it or not, Conrad belongs with Yeats, Joyce and Eliot as a modern master of the mythico-historical pun. He shared their obsession with history and in particular their belief that the linear-progressive view of history is a grave obstacle to man's understanding of himself; like them, he sought in consequence to show that the forms of contemporary experience are reincarnations of historical and mythical paradigms.

The Limits of Irony

Martin Price

In *Nostromo* Conrad's irony becomes more inclusive, enfolding the political history of a nation as well as the motives of individuals. The central irony is that of "material interests." They alone seem to possess the power to bring order to Costaguana. They require stability for their profitable operation, and they bring peace through their great financial power, through bribery or an improved standard of living. The danger of "material interests," in turn, lies in their use of the power they acquire, making men instruments of an institution and sacrificing them when they fail to be useful.

The story of the Gould concession opens in Italy, where Charles and Emilia meet. She is staying with an old aunt, the widow of an Italian nobleman who gave his life in Garibaldi's cause. The *marchesa* now leads "a still, whispering existence" in a part of "an ancient and ruinous palace, whose big empty halls downstairs sheltered under their painted ceilings the harvests, the fowls, and even the cattle, together with the whole family of the tenant farmer." It is there that Charles brings the news of his father's death. The death has been caused by the torment of the unworked silver mine, whose ownership Mr. Gould has not been allowed to relinquish and for which he has been forced to pay a stiff annual fee. It has been a grotesque but fatal farce. Charles and Emilia meet "in the hall of the ruined *palazzo*, a room magnificent and naked, with here and there a long strip of damask, black with damp and age, hanging down on a bare panel of the wall. It was furnished with exactly one gilt armchair, with a broken back, and an octagon

From *Forms of Life: Character and Moral Imagination in the Novel.* © 1983 by Yale University. Yale University Press, 1983.

columnar stand bearing a heavy marble vase ornamented with sculptured masks and garlands of flowers, and cracked from top to bottom." Charles stares at the urn as he speaks and kisses her hand. Emilia weeps in sympathy, "very small in her simple, white frock, almost like a lost child crying in the degraded grandeur of the noble hall, while he stood by her, again perfectly motionless in the contemplation of the marble urn"(part 1, chap. 6).

Conrad uses the setting of the palazzo to suggest the world the Goulds will enter, the "degraded grandeur" comprehending both the original idealism with which their silver mine will be worked and the long history of corruptibility to which Gould's service to material interests will add another chapter. One can both recognize the Goulds' new hope as they stand in the decayed palazzo and read, in the painted ceiling above them, the grandeur of an older generation which has had to yield to fowls and cattle its uselessly large and formal spaces. Conrad does not insist upon allegorical meanings, but he exacts from his scene a high degree of initial suggestion and of ultimate relevance. Some of it is perhaps apparent at once to Charles, who stares at the cracked urn "as though he had resolved to fix its shape forever in his memory." But it is not clear what he sees. The scene, garrulous with suggestion for us, like the sounding church bell "thin and alert" in the valley below, is something of which the Goulds are perhaps touchingly, even pathetically, oblivious. They are excited now by a future "in which there was an air of adventure, of combat—a subtle thought of redress and conquest." It is a prospect which earns for Charles Gould an ironic comment which he does not hear and could hardly imagine: "Action is consolatory. It is the enemy of thought and the friend of flattering illusions. Only in the conduct of our action can we find the sense of mastery over the Fates" (part 1, chap. 6).

The enthusiasm with which Emilia later speaks of the mine, deprecating her genuine idealism with a "slight flavor of irony," charms visitors to the Casa Gould; but it does not lead them to imagine any higher end than the acquisition of wealth. The betrayal of Emilia's idealism and its faint pathos are suggested by the niche in the steps of their house where a Madonna stands "with the crowned child sitting on her arm." More visible and audible is the "big green parrot, brilliant like an emerald in a cage that flashed like gold." Like the player piano in *The Secret Agent* or its ancestor, Mrs. Merdle's derisive parrot in *Little Dorrit*, the parrot performs at irregular intervals; it sometimes screams out "Viva Costaguana," or calls the servant "mellifluously . . . in imitation of Mrs. Gould's voice," or as suddenly takes "refuge in immobility and silence."

The Goulds feel "morally bound to make good their vigourous view of life against the unnatural error of weariness and despair." In order to accomplish this, Charles Gould needs the financial support of Holroyd, an American millionaire with "the temperament of a puritan and an insatiable imagination of conquest." Holroyd wants to conquer the world for the "purer forms of Christianity" and for American business; the two goals are fused in the cant of a ruthless idealism. It is not the only idealism Charles Gould encounters outside his own. Another version is the republican eloquence and vision of freedom of Antonia's father, Don José Avellanos. Emilia Gould thinks Charles muddleheaded for equating the two forms of idealism, but Charles has the confidence of a man convinced of his own realism. Others may declaim, he says, "but I pin my faith to material interests." He has, he thinks, no illusions; he is "prepared to stoop for his weapons" (part 1, chap. 6).

During the years of her travel in Costaguana with her husband, Emilia Gould has come to know the land beyond the coastal settlements, "a great land of plain and mountain and people, suffering and mute, waiting for the future in a pathetic immobility of patience." Everywhere she finds "a weary desire for peace, the dread of officialdom with its nightmarish parody administration without law, without security, and without justice" (part 1, chap. 7). The history of Costaguana has been a grotesque succession of forms of power, some barbarous, some virtuous but weak, none stable for long; it is a history of contingency, of upset and overturn, with only the misery of the people a constant presence beneath the various forms that oppression may take. Charles Gould puts up with idiocy and venality; he lives within a fortress of polite silence. The land has changed as the mine has grown; the original waterfall of San Tomé survives only as a memory in Emilia Gould's watercolor sketch. Emilia keeps alive the idealism she has shared with Charles: "she endowed that lump of metal"—the first silver ingot produced by the mine—"with a justificative conception, as though it were not a mere fact, but something far-reaching and unpalpable, like the true expression of an emotion or the emergence of a principle" (part 1, chap. 8). But Emilia becomes at last an ineffectual and lonely spectator, dismayed by the weight of power that the mine carries in the new political state of its own creation, Sulaco.

Dr. Monygham, who shares her vision, is another bitter spectator. He has learned, he thinks, to live without illusions; his self-respect had been destroyed under torture when he found himself betraying others to the dictator, Guzman Bento. Like Lord Jim, he is "the slave of a ghost," haunted by his failure. He has created "an ideal conception of his disgrace," not a false reading of the past but "a rule of conduct resting mainly on severe

rejections." Dr. Monygham's "eminently loyal nature" can trust only someone so innocent and helpless as Emilia Gould. For her husband's efforts he
has only scorn:

> The administrador had acted as if the immense and powerful
> prosperity of the mine had been founded on methods of probity,
> on the sense of usefulness. And it was nothing of the kind. The
> method followed had been the only one possible. The Gould
> Concession had ransomed its way through all those years. It was
> a nauseous process. He quite understood that Charles Gould had
> got sick of it and had left the old path to back up that hopeless
> attempt at reform. The doctor did not believe in the reform of
> Costaguana. . . . What made him uneasy was that Charles Gould
> seemed to him to have weakened at the decisive moment when a
> frank return to the old methods was the only chance. Listening
> to Decoud's wild scheme had been a weakness.
>
> (part 3, chap. 4)

This passage is interesting as much for the moral confusion it embodies as
for that which it attacks. Charles Gould is blamed for pretending to high
purpose while using base means. Could he have exercised it more fully by
some other means? No, his method was "the only one possible," but we
must recognize it for what it is. Charles Gould has in fact tried to free himself of the base methods; his very eagerness to do so led to his support of so
weak a reformer as Ribiera. Would it have been better both to practice base
means and renounce a high purpose? This would seem to Dr. Monygham
more sensible since the high purpose of reform was, in his eyes, fordoomed.
And now Dr. Monygham is troubled because Gould turns to Decoud's plan
for an independent Sulaco instead of using his silver, as he has before, to buy
off the latest would-be Caesars, the Montero brothers. As we see, Gould is
more realistic in this than Dr. Monygham.

One is left with a morality that scorns bribery but scolds Gould for
repudiating it, that questions Gould's success but fears his failure; it is a
morality that can question any action since its grounds for judgment shift
between an exacting idealism and a cynical despair. Any form of success
must be unthinkable for Dr. Monygham, and any apparent success must
reveal itself to be a new and more insidious form of failure. Only the commitment to personal loyalty survives the larger pattern of Dr. Monygham's
fatalism. The doctor is loyal to the mine because it "presented itself . . . in
the shape of a little woman, . . . the delicate preciousness of her inner worth,
partaking of a gem and a flower, revealed in every attitude of her person."

In the presence of danger "this illusion acquired force, permanency, and authority. It claimed him at last!" Dr. Monygham's loyalty to Mrs. Gould is as ruthless as any of the illusions we see in the novel: it steels him "against remorse and pity" (part 3, chap. 8). As he undertakes deception in her cause, he feels that he is "the only one fit for that dirty work." Like Lord Jim, Dr. Monygham feels disabled by his failure; he "believed that he had forfeited the right to be indignant with any one — for anything." It is only the "exaltation of self-sacrifice" that can support him.

Martin Decoud, different as he is from Dr. Monygham, shares his distrust of Charles Gould's unstable mixture of moral idealism and material interests. The distrust comes in each case, I would argue, from a deeper idealism that each tries to disguise as (or reduce to) a personal loyalty. Decoud does not have Monygham's shame of betrayal (or, in Dickens's phrase, his "vanity of unworthiness"). Decoud seems, as we first encounter him, a supercilious young expatriate, a smatterer in satiric journalism, a man who prefers the boulevards of Paris to the barbarism of his own country. He is torn between a despair of ever bringing order to Costaguana and the infamy of serving interests whose motives or whose realism he can easily impugn.

Decoud suffers from a kind of spoiled idealism; he cannot admit impurity of motive without feeling betrayed and controlled by it. Antonia, who does not suffer from the same fastidiousness, rejects his cynicism: "Men must be used as they are. I suppose nobody is really disinterested, unless, perhaps, you, Don Martin." For whenever Decoud puts aside an idealistic goal (which he nevertheless uses as a touchstone of others' actions), he reverts to a cynicism which seems to take people at their worst. "You read all the correspondence, you write all the papers," he says to Antonia, "all those state papers that are inspired here, in this room, in blind deference to a theory of political purity." But Gould's company and his mine are the "practical demonstrations" of what is possible. "Do you think he succeeded by his fidelity to a theory of virtue?" And yet, for all the guilt he may have incurred, Gould has been too weak to carry bribery far enough to buy off the Monteros (part 1, chap. 5).

Decoud professes himself unmoved by the claims of patriotism; such "narrowness" of belief must be "odious" to "cultured minds." But at a deeper level, Decoud seems bitterly disappointed in his country, where patriotism has too often been "the cry of dark barbarism, the cloak of lawlessness, of crime, of rapacity, or simple thieving." Even as he denounces Costaguana, Decoud is "surprised at the warmth" of his own words. Antonia picks up that point: "The word you despise has stood also for courage, for constancy, for suffering." Decoud cannot accede to Antonia's faith: for him a conviction remains only a "particular view of personal advantage either practical or emotional." He rejects patriotic illusions. He claims "only the supreme illusion of a lover." This is Decoud's form of authenticity. He can accept none of the hypocrisy, the self-deception, or fanaticism he sees in Costaguanan patriotism; he holds to a principle he can acknowledge as quixotic but also as personal and sincere.

In political affairs Decoud has cultivated detachment: he "imagined himself to derive an artistic pleasure from watching the picturesque extreme of wrongheadedness into which an honest, almost sacred, conviction may drive a man." It seems to Decoud that every conviction, to the extent that it is effective, becomes delusion or madness; the man who has come to accept a belief is no longer in command of it or himself. But while he regards himself as a connoisseur of madness, enjoying the colorful virulence of others' obsessions, he tries to preserve decency in skepticism. He deposits in his skeptical better self the full awareness he must relinquish as a propagandist. His better self preserves its integrity, and he wishes it to remain an asylum, an eventual place of return for the activist, the ideologist and propagandist, he finds himself becoming (part 1, chap. 5).

Decoud can participate in action only by scorning the limitations—he would say dishonesty—that action imposes. Yet some of his best feelings, concealed from his ironic consciousness as they must be to survive, are at work in his political action. Emilia Gould sees a "tremendous excitement under its cloak of studied carelessness," betrayed in "his audacious and watchful stare, in the curve, half-reckless, half-contemptuous, of his lips." Nevertheless, he mocks his own enthusiasm as he proposes that Sulaco secede and become a new state. His devotion to the new cause is born, he insists, of love for Antonia rather than any idealism of Charles Gould's kind. Gould, he insists to Emilia, "cannot act or exist without idealizing every simple feeling, desire, or achievement" (part 2, chap. 6).

Decoud wants no such sublimation. He ascribes it to Antonia, and it clearly has some part in her appeal for him; but he thinks he undertakes the cause he has devised only to be able to remain with her (since, he adds mockingly, she refuses to run away). While Decoud scorns Gould's "senti-mental basis for action," he appeals nevertheless to Emilia Gould's concern for the victims she has protected: "Are you not responsible to your con-science for all these people? Is it not worthwile to make another effort, which is not at all so desperate as it looks?" Yet, having said this, Decoud must separate himself from her husband's idealism. "I cannot endow my personal desires with a shining robe of silk and jewels," he boasts. "Life is not for me a moral romance derived from the tradition of a pretty fairy tale." With the supremely ironic blindness of the self-styled realist, Decoud asserts, "I am not afraid of my motives."

At the mention by Mrs. Gould of the banker Holroyd, Decoud comes to a second plan—not only to create an independent state of Sulaco but to save the next shipment of silver from capture by the Monteros. In effect, he accepts the material interests in the simplest sense of that phrase: "This silver must be kept flowing north to return in the form of financial backing from the great house of Holroyd." For the task of saving the silver Decoud thinks of Nostromo. He trusts Nostromo's self-interest; Nostromo came to Costaguana, by his own account, to seek his fortune. Emilia puts her trust in Nostromo's integrity; old Viola has called him "the incorruptible." "I prefer," she says to Decoud, "to think him disinterested, and therefore trustworthy." Neither of them can quite imagine Nostromo's vanity and his dependence upon others' regard (part 2, chap. 6).

Nostromo is neither mercenary nor idealistic in the ways that they imagine. As Teresa Viola recognizes, he is under the spell of his reputation, eager to gain distinction by being "invaluable" to people like Captain Mitchell. He is precisely opposed to old Giorgio Viola, in whom the "spirit of self-forgetfulness, the simple devotion to a vast humanitarian idea" has bred "an austere contempt for all personal advantage." Viola cries out fiercely in behalf of Garibaldi's followers: "We wanted nothing, we suffered for the love of all humanity!" (part 1, chap. 4). Nostromo has little of this thoughtful idealism; he is the captive of an image rather than of an idea. It is a handsome image. We see it best in the swaggering performance with which he turns off the anger of a pretty *morenita* and allows her to cut the silver buttons from his coat.

Whereas Charles Gould is a captive of an idea and an institution, Nostromo becomes the captive of the literal silver. Doomed to possess it, daring to spend it only very slowly, unable to return it because of the missing bars with which Decoud weighted his body, he becomes "the slave of a treasure with full self-knowledge" (part 2, chap. 12). He must live by stealth and suffer a disabling sense of falseness, and he feels at the last that the silver has killed him. As she comforts Giselle Viola, who loved Nostromo, Emilia Gould has the "first and only moment of bitterness in her life," and speaks in terms worthy of Dr. Monygham himself: "Console yourself, child. Very soon he would have forgotten you for his treasure" (part 3, chap. 13). In effect, as Emilia Gould recognizes, Nostromo transposes the pattern of Charles Gould to another key. Nostromo turns out to be a far less interesting, far less complex character than he promises to be at first, and that is true of Gould as well. This has been explained by H. M. Daleski as the "thwarting of the conventional expectations" awakened by the characters and the mine itself. Just as the idealism is replaced by impoverishing obsession, so these characters have less and less life.

With studied irony, Conrad allows Captain Mitchell to introduce us to the new state of Sulaco. His naive pride in the new republic is the means by which we learn how the events initiated by the doctor and Nostromo have concluded. He provides a requiem for the heroic dead and an altogether uncritical account of how heroism and dedication have been absorbed into new institutional structures. Father Corbelán is now a cardinal-archbishop. Hernandez, who was once a kind of Robin Hood, a glorious outlaw, is now minister of war. Even Dr. Monygham has an institutional role as inspector of state hospitals. The war to free Sulaco has been ended by an "international naval demonstration" in the harbor; a United States cruiser was the first to give official recognition to the new state. Once more Conrad has forced together the heroism in which the state is conceived with the bureaucratic structure and scene of imperialist enterprise it becomes.

The next stage of Sulaco's history is suggested in the doctor's conversation with Antonia Avellanos and Father Corbelán. They are now involved in promoting a campaign to annex the rest of Costaguana to the new power of Sulaco. For Antonia this would be a means of using the wealth of the new state to relieve the oppression of fellow countrymen. Dr. Monygham ridicules this hope: "Yes, but the material interests will not let you jeopardize their development for a mere idea of pity and justice." He characteristically adds: "And it is just as well perhaps." The true support for Antonia's hope has been found in "the secret societies amongst immigrants and natives, where Nostromo . . . is the great man." Such a movement, Dr. Monygham adds, may simply exploit the appeal of "the wealth for the people." With all his cynicism about both forces, Dr. Monygham expects violence:

> "There is no place and no rest in the development of material interests. They have their law, and their justice. But it is founded on expediency, and is inhuman; it is without rectitude, without the continuity and the force that can be found only in a moral principle. Mrs. Gould, the time approaches when all that the Gould Concession stands for shall weigh as heavily upon the people as the barbarism, cruelty, and misrule of a few years back."

It will "provoke resentment, bloodshed, and vengeance, because the men have grown different." Does this mean simply that men will become disaffected with the mine or does it imply that they have now acquired higher expectations of their worth and rights? (part 3, chap. 11).

What are we to make of Dr. Monygham and Emilia Gould? They lack the "polished callousness" or even the simple worldliness that might make for tolerance of the mixed motive or belief in its usefulness. He is a man of deep feeling, whose vulnerability creates "his sardonic turn of mind and his biting speeches." He shares Emilia's "still and sad immobility." Both accept the fatality of forces that have been released and can no longer be recalled. Mrs. Gould's nightmare vision is of an "immense desolation" in which she survives alone "the degradation of her young ideal of life, of love, of work —all alone in the Treasure House of the World." Both have the moral intensity of quietism. Emilia Gould thinks: "There was something inherent in the necessities of successful action which carried with it the moral degradation of the idea" (part 3, chap. 11). The alternatives to the process are either unsuccessful action or none at all. There may be a grandeur of despair in such an assertion that compensates for the inability to act. Not to act is at least to commit no error and do no wrong. It leaves the realm of politics to one or another pattern of fanaticism or cynicism. In *Nostromo* there are intimations of a new radical, perhaps revolutionary, movement, emerging under the cover of Nostromo's leadership but under the real direction of "an indigent, sickly, somewhat hunchbacked little photographer, with a white face and a magnanimous soul dyed crimson by a bloodthirsty hate of all capitalists, oppressors of the two hemispheres" (part 3, chap. 12). Rarely has a magnanimous soul been so poorly housed and so passively governed by rage.

I have tried to get at the way in which Conrad's tendency to reduce experience to the outrage of an impossible choice requires characters of a special kind. In *Lord Jim* the puzzle surrounds the hero. He is generously conceived, neither shown as master of his fate nor made a moral bankrupt. Marlow in turn is a figure of fuller consciousness, deeply concerned with the questions which Jim exemplifies but which Marlow alone can formulate. Marlow fails to save Jim; he can only observe the destiny Jim achieves once he goes to Patusan. And the initial hope gives way to something darker and enigmatic. In *Nostromo* Conrad has created characters who are victims of an idea. We see that theme announced early: the "cool purity" of the white peak of Higuerota—a "colossal embodiment of silence"—seems to fade into (Conrad is very cinematic) the white hair of the anachronistic old Garibaldino Giorgio Viola. Charles Gould pursues an idea which requires means that threaten to subvert its end; his failure lies in his uncritical commitment to "material interests," and that is in turn reflected in the dehumanization imposed upon him by the idea. His "subtle conjugal infidelity" to Emilia is like Jim's to Jewel—each man turns to an idea as to "an Eastern bride" who has come "veiled to his side." In Jim's case it is "a pitiless wedding with a shadowy ideal of conduct"; in Gould's with a sense of "redress and conquest." Conrad stresses the futility of Gould's achievement: the peace of the Sulaco we come to under the guidance of Captain Mitchell is made, like that of Geneva in *Under Western Eyes*, to seem complacent and indifferent to the claims of any idea. It is at most a superficial peace, for the promise of new violence is inherent in the dialectic of material interests.

What I miss is some intimation of men being moved by mixed motives without inevitably succumbing to the lowest. There seems at moments something rigged in Conrad's demonstration of futility, of the impossibility of Costaguana's ever achieving a government both tolerable and stable. It is not hard to be realistic if one rules out hope, and it is not hard to be ironic—it is in fact hard not to be—if all forms of political activity lead to the same inevitable futility. Unlimited irony can easily turn into fatalism.

Decoud, we are told by the author, "died from solitude and want of faith in himself and others." Solitude creates "a state of soul in which the affectations of irony and scepticism have no place." Decoud can no longer set himself against the world but is absorbed into it at the cost of his identity. "In our activity alone do we find the sustaining illusion of an independent existence as against the whole scheme of things of which we form a helpless part" (part 3, chap. 10). The fatalism of "form a helpless part" and the skepticism of "sustaining illusion" make one wonder whether a novelist who writes these words would succumb, or fear that he might succumb, as Decoud does. One recalls Conrad's words about writing *Lord Jim*: "Everything is there: descriptions, dialogue, reflexion—everything—everything but the belief, the conviction, the only thing needed to make me put pen to paper."

Many have felt that Conrad is trying to exorcise something by forcing himself to imagine his way into Decoud—just as there were moments in the writing of *The Secret Agent* when he was, as he tells us, an "extreme revolutionist." If Decoud is a "victim of the disillusioned weariness which is the retribution meted out to intellectual audacity," he seems a thinner character in his death than in his life. One may feel that he is not so much "swallowed up in the immense indifference of things" as sentenced and executed by his author. I wonder why so few are ready to question the propriety of Decoud's suicide, to ask, that is, whether it seems an action that follows from his nature rather than a somewhat superstitious reprisal against the irony and skepticism that the author otherwise overindulges.

But the problem of Decoud is only part of what seems to me troublesome in the novel. As I have indicated, the central characters are captivated by "illusion," with little capacity to recognize or resist it; or, if they are without illusion, they are without power or hope as well. The book achieves some tragic force. It does not achieve that force by demonstrating the inevitable corruption and the implicit blindness of all action, at least of all action that professes a purpose or an ideal. For Conrad's feelings are truer than his thought. There is more complexity in his presentation of characters than there is in his analysis; and, if we see more in what they do than Conrad's ironic handling allows for, it is because they have won their claims upon our minds and feelings in those unattended moments when Conrad's oversight allows them some freedom.

Four Views of the Hero

Stephen K. Land

The pattern of Gould's career so far [prior to joining the separatist movement] has followed that of the early heroes Almayer and Willems, men whose purposive action places them in a world of dualistic conflict, in which every deliberate step they take towards their goal involves deeper compromise and further entanglement in the universal struggle. Like them, Gould identifies his ideal with a heroine, with whom, after an initial period of unison, he finds himself increasingly at odds; and like them he finds himself opposed in his efforts by a man from within the world he has selected for his sphere of operations, a rival whose enmity is provoked by the hero's very successes. We would therefore expect, all other things being equal, that towards the end of the story the growing tension would snap and Gould would be confronted, probably with fatal result, by the consequences of his compromises, as are Almayer and Willems and all the heroes of the intervening novels. Yet this does not happen in *Nostromo*. Not only does Gould survive the end of the story, but he defeats his rival, Montero, and succeeds in his separatist venture.

Gould's impunity does not mean that Conrad has changed his view of the human situation to allow his hero to evade the usual nemesis. Gould is still in action at the end of the story because *Nostromo* is uniquely structured among Conrad's works and because Gould is not the sole hero of the story. The end of the book centres not upon Gould but on Nostromo, who does complete the normal cycle from compromise to destruction, while Gould, after the decision to pursue separatism, is kept all but invisible in the back-

---

From *Conrad and the Paradox of Plot*. © 1984 by Stephen K. Land. Macmillan, 1984.

ground. *Nostromo*, furthermore, while taking its plot from a short slice of time, is full of both allusions to the past and hints of the future. It portrays, rather like the Wagnerian story, one turn of a cycle that might be indefinitely repeated. For this reason it is impossible to select a single event with which the story "begins"; the granting of the Concession, the decision of Charles Gould to disregard his father's warning, the alliance with Holroyd, the adoption or the failure of Ribierism could all be put forward for the position with more or less equal plausibility. In a similar way, although the story stops with the death of Nostromo, it does not really "end" there, as the main political sequence of events, in which Gould has become inextricably involved, is still very much in motion.

We are told, for instance, that after the political separation and the establishment of a government consistent with Gould's ideas there grows up a democratic opposition made up chiefly from Italians and natives, former employees of the railway and of the mine itself. At the same time, some of Gould's political allies are saying that the logical and necessary conclusion of their work must be the annexation of the rest of Costaguana to the new state, and that the democratic party is lending its support to this view. Clearly, as Monygham observes, "there is no peace and no rest in the development of material interests." The silver of the mine is like Wagner's gold; it cannot allow the world in which it is at large to rest stable, but is always at work to keep the balance of forces swinging.

Gould will not, therefore, be allowed to enjoy for long the momentary success of his latest compromise. The new state is, by the time the story closes, already looking towards its next crisis, a choice between widespread internal discontent and a war of annexation, a selection of paths from which Gould will be unable to hold aloof. Gould's nemesis is not avoided, but merely suspended by the end of the novel.

In yet another sense, however, Gould pays the price of his concession to material interests even within the pages of the story, for towards the end he becomes plainly the prisoner of the mine rather than its master and has lost his relationship with Emilia. Emilia herself gives us the final picture of Gould.

> She had a clear vision of the gray hairs on his temples. He was perfect—perfect. What more could she have expected? It was a colossal and lasting success; and love was only a short moment of forgetfulness, a short intoxication, whose delight one remembered with a sense of sadness, as if it had been a deep grief lived through. There was something inherent in the necessities of successful action which carried with it the moral degradation of the

idea. . . . He was perfect, perfect; but she would never have him to herself. . . . [S]he saw clearly the San Tomé mine possessing, consuming, burning up the life of the last of the Costaguana Goulds; mastering the spirit of the son as it had mastered the lamentable weakness of the father. A terrible success for the last of the Goulds.

Emilia sees, as in a way she has seen from the beginning, the fate towards which Gould is heading as a logical result of his decision to return to Costaguana and his willingness to compromise.

While Gould's end remains below the horizon at the conclusion of *Nostromo*, another character, Martin Decoud, is seen to complete the full Conradian heroic cycle from initial compromise through paradox to fateful nemesis. Decoud, although he enters the story at a point after its beginning (when he returns from Europe to his native Costaguana to help support the declining Ribierist cause) and dies well before its end, is one of the novel's four focal figures. Like Gould, Nostromo and Monygham, Decoud acts independently at a crucial stage so as to affect the course of the plot and cannot therefore be viewed as a minor character subordinate to some other hero.

Decoud's character has two salient features; he is a sceptic and is also an adept in the use of words. In this lies the particular form of the paradox which engulfs him, for his fate is to become a literary propagandist, a spinner of words, while at the same time believing nothing of the doctrines he expounds.

Like the other heroes, Gould, Nostromo and Monygham, Decoud is personally an outsider, a man of European culture and racial background, although, like Gould, he has a family history of settlement in Costaguana. When we first hear of him Decoud, like Gould, is in Europe, with the option of remaining uninvolved in the affairs of the South American republic. He engages himself in these affairs, however, largely because of Antonia, the devoted daughter of José Avellanos, a noted Costaguana statesman and patriot. Antonia is for Decoud, much as Emilia is for Gould, an ideal woman under whose influence begins his involvement with Costaguana. Decoud arrives in Sulaco in connection with an arms deal he has been negotiating on his travels, but after a reunion with Antonia he abandons his intention of continuing on his way and elects to remain, allowing himself to be recruited by her father to the liberal cause.

Antonia is therefore, from Decoud's point of view, the heroine of the story. Like other Conradian heroines, from Nina and Aissa through Jewel to Emilia Gould, Antonia represents both something to which the hero aspires and something which, by his very nature, he is debarred from attaining. Emilia represents the humanitarian aspect of Gould's idealism, but is increasingly separated from him by the means he employs in pursuit of these goals. Antonia attracts Decoud by her European outlook and education, her emancipation and freedom of thought which make her his natural partner.

> Antonia could hold her own in a discussion with two or three men at a time. Obviously she was not the girl to be content with peeping through a barred window at a cloaked figure of a lover ensconced in a doorway opposite—which is the correct form of Costaguana courtship. It was generally believed that with her foreign upbringing and foreign ideas the learned and proud Antonia would never marry—unless, indeed, she married a foreigner from Europe or North America, now that Sulaco seemed on the point of being invaded by all the world.

Decoud shares her foreignness, something of her pride, and much of the European orientation cultivated by her father. Yet he is barred from her by his scepticism which prevents him from sharing unreservedly in her Costaguana patriotism and devotion to the Ribierist cause. The situation which therefore develops between them is comparable to that between Willems and Aissa; each finds much to admire in the other, but the woman is bound to a country and people where the man finds himself threatened in body and stifled in spirit.

Decoud compromises at first by deciding to remain with Antonia in Costaguana and by adopting her family's politics, currently expressed in fanatical support of the Ribierist cause. To this end he becomes "the Journalist of Sulaco" by Don José's appointment, taking control of a newspaper christened the *Porvenir*. The irony of this undertaking lies not in the mere journalism (which Decoud had practised occasionally in Europe) but in the fact that the *Porvenir* is a political organ committed unreservedly to the liberal doctrines backed by Avellanos and Gould, in which doctrines, by and large, Decoud has no faith.

Having compromised and involved himself in local affairs for the heroine's sake, Decoud, like Willems, finds that his own survival is threatened by his adopted environment. As an intelligent and sensitive man, although unable to accept Costaguana politics at face value, he is disturbed by the strife and suffering it generates.

> The reality of the political action, such as it was, seemed closer, and acquired poignancy by Antonia's belief in the cause. Its crudeness hurt his feelings. He was surprised at his own sensitiveness.

"I suppose I am more of a Costaguanero than I could have believed possible," he thought to himself.

His disdain grew like a reaction of his scepticism against the action into which he was forced by his infatuation for Antonia.

At the same time, again like Willems, he is placing himself in physical danger of reprisal by his action on behalf of the heroine's party. The paradox is clear; he is unable to live without Antonia, but in remaining with her he endangers his mental and bodily survival.

Decoud's solution would be to take Antonia away from Costaguana, which is just what he wishes to do. "He also had his aspirations, he aspired to carry her away out of these deadly futilities of pronunciamentos and reforms." He is prevented by her ties to the country and by her liberal patriotism, both imaged in her devotion to her father, who is himself the focal point of the "pronunciamentos and reforms" which Decoud sees as "utterly wrong." Avellanos therefore appears, with respect to Decoud, in the role of the rival, the figure who opposes the resolution of the hero's difficulties with the heroine, much as Montero, the enemy of Ribierism, becomes the rival of Gould.

Although there is no personal animosity in this particular rivalry, Avellanos, the effective force binding Antonia to Costaguana, is in several significant ways the very antithesis of Decoud. Where Decoud is a sceptic without allegiances, Avellanos is a patriot and a passionate believer in "the doctrine of political rectitude"; and whereas Decoud becomes a writer only under protest, Avellanos is already the author of a large exposition of his ideas in the light of the history of his country. Avellanos, moreover, is a professional diplomat, while Decoud exhibits the artistic intellectual's contempt for political machinations.

> Don José Avellanos desired passionately for his country: peace, prosperity, and (as the end of the preface to "Fifty Years of Misrule" has it) "an honourable place in the comity of civilized nations." In this last phrase the Minister Plenipotentiary, cruelly humiliated by the bad faith of his government towards the foreign bondholders, stands disclosed in the patriot.

Structurally, therefore, Avellanos stands opposed to Decoud much as does Omar to Willems, being the heroine's father, representing an orthodox spirit alien to the hero, and preventing, by his very existence, the satisfactory union of the lovers.

Decoud's response is the Conradian hero's characteristic decision to immerse in the "destructive element" of his compromise. Since he can neither take Antonia out of Costaguana nor remain contentedly with her under the existing conditions, he resolves to alter the conditions by committing himself further and taking a directive part in local affairs. He devises and promulgates the idea of separatism, the political movement which will dissociate the western province from the rest of the country and thereby, he hopes, end Antonia's involvement in the degradation of Costaguana politics. He explains his idea to Emilia with particular lucidity: "She [Antonia] won't leave Sulaco for my sake, therefore Sulaco must leave the rest of the Republic to its fate. . . . I cannot part with Antonia, therefore the one and indivisible Republic of Costaguana must be made to part with its western province. Fortunately it happens to be also a sound policy."

The idea of separation is directly "contrary to the doctrine laid down in the 'History of Fifty Years' Misrule.'" The Avellanos patriotism encompasses the whole country and cannot easily contemplate the dismemberment of Costaguana. Just as Omar in *An Outcast of the Islands* dies at the point of Willems's triumphant introduction of the Arabs to Sambir, so Avellanos is effectively killed by the adoption and success of Decoud's separatist doctrine. His unwilling expression from his deathbed of consent to this move is his last action.

Despite the collapse of his rival, however, Decoud is still enmeshed in a paradoxical situation. The first essential to the preservation of the western province as a political entity is the removal of the latest consignment of silver from the mine, which will otherwise fall into the hands of the Monterists. As the originator of the separatist policy, it is right that Decoud himself should oversee this operation, while at the same time his own safety dictates his temporary departure from Sulaco, threatened as it is by Montero's oncoming forces. Decoud therefore accompanies Nostromo, taking the lighter of silver out into the Gulf under cover of darkness, and finds himself once again separated from Antonia.

The lighter is struck in the darkness by Sotillo's troopship. Nostromo manages to bring it safely to the Great Isabel (an island in the Gulf), where he hides the treasure and leaves Decoud, intending to return when he has made contact with his friends in Sulaco. But for various reasons Nostromo does not return, and Decoud, unable to bear the solitude, commits suicide by jumping into the sea weighted with bars of silver. There is therefore no nemesis character involved in Decoud's end, which is self-inflicted in an isolation caused by a sequence of accidents, but the imagery surrounding the event is precisely sculpted to the pattern of the usual Conradian heroic catastrophe. Decoud, as a sceptic who has compromised by becoming involved in Costaguana politics, is cast adrift in the Gulf when he is struck by a native troopship on a political errand. The drifting in the Gulf reflects the former aimlessness of his existence, while the collision is an obvious representation of the liabilities entailed by his compromise. His solitude on the island is emblematic of his deliberate intellectual aloofness from human affairs, the logical conclusion of his sceptical disavowal of all commitment. Decoud's nemesis, the solitude of the Costaguana Gulf, is therefore a typical Conradian end, in which the hero is fatally confronted with the extreme implications of his own conduct. As Brown is to Jim, Jones to Heyst, so is the solitude of the Gulf to Decoud.

> Solitude from mere outward condition of existence becomes very swiftly a state of soul in which the affectations of irony and scepticism have no place. It takes possession of the mind, and drives forth the thought into the exile of utter unbelief. After three days of waiting for the sight of some human face, Decoud caught himself entertaining a doubt of his own individuality. . . . On the fifth day an immense melancholy descended upon him palpably. . . . His sadness was the sadness of a sceptical mind. He beheld the universe as a succession of incomprehensible images.

In this frame of mind, driven to ultimate disbelief, Decoud shoots himself and drops into the Gulf.

The solitude of the Gulf which kills Decoud is an image also of the separationist policy, for on the Great Isabel Decoud himself experiences the extreme of separation. The marooning and death of Decoud show that separatism, although genuinely beneficial to the western province, is tainted with immoral selfishness and therefore ultimately moribund, both in that it is conceived by Decoud for a selfish reason (to secure the company of Antonia) and in that (as Antonia herself later realizes) it involves the casting off of a larger and poorer part of the country. Typically Decoud dies from an excessive application of the principles involved in his own compromise. The silver ingots which weigh down his body signify the material, selfish aspect of the separatist policy, of which the treasure was to have been a key instrument.

The treasure is also instrumental in the scheme of Dr. Monygham, whose career similarly exhibits aspects of the Conradian heroic pattern. His nature is itself paradoxical, in that he is at once both a confirmed pessimist, taking an exceedingly cynical view of humanity, and a dedicated humanitarian, deeply sensitive to the sufferings and misfortunes of others. His cynicism evidently rests upon his own past experience of political persecution, captivity and torture, in the course of which, it is said, he made extorted confessions implicating many of his fellows.

> His confessions, when they came at last, were very complete, too. Sometimes on the nights when he walked the floor, he won-dered, grinding his teeth with shame and rage, at the fertility of his imagination when stimulated by a sort of pain which makes truth, honour, self-respect, and life itself matters of little moment.

This grim confrontation with his own weakness makes of the Doctor a severe judge of the motives of others, and in the grossly acquisitive and unprincipled context of Costaguana politics he finds himself at odds with every other major character in the story, excepting only Emilia, whose unaffected and selfless charity he idealizes.

Monygham's obsession with his disgrace drives him, after another political revolution has brought about his abrupt release, to a self-imposed isolation from European society. Like the other heroes of the story, he is not a native Costaguanero but is of European family, and for him, as for the others, loss of European characteristics under the exigencies of the local situation is generally significant of moral decline. When released from prison Monygham is physically decrepit and dressed in a comical parody of native costume.

> And these conditions seemed to bind him indissolubly to the land of Costaguana like an awful procedure of naturalization, involv-ing him deep in the national life, far deeper than any amount of success and honour could have done. They did away with his Europeanism; for Dr. Monygham had made himself an ideal conception of his disgrace.

Thus "bound" to native evils Monygham becomes, to a large extent by his own choice, an "outcast" from European society in Sulaco.

Monygham is, none the less, a man of great compassion, as is shown generally by his performance of medical duties and, in particular, by his care of such individuals as the Violas. His rough cynicism is, in fact, the product of his insight into suffering and an expression of contempt for those who ignore it. It is therefore natural that he should turn to Emilia, the only character of uncompromising humanity in the story, and one who shares his concern for the basic welfare of the common people. Emilia therefore be-comes his heroine. "He believed her worthy of every devotion." And by the same token Gould, who appears to Monygham to have sacrificed Emilia's happiness and to have imperilled the safety of the workers for the sake of material interests, is his hated rival.

In pursuit of his ideal Monygham effects a compromise. In order to win Emilia's friendship and, through her, the post of medical officer, he makes a partial reentry into the European society he had previously abandoned, and from any true sympathy with which he is still debarred by his outlook. As with Gould and Nostromo, the state of Monygham's dress again illuminates the compromise.

> Had it not been for the immaculate cleanliness of his apparel he might have been taken for one of those shiftless Europeans that are a moral eyesore to the respectability of a foreign colony in almost every exotic part of the world. The young ladies of Sulaco, adorning with clusters of pretty faces the balconies along the Street of the Constitution, when they saw him pass, with his limping gait and bowed head, a short linen jacket drawn on carelessly over the flannel check shirt, would remark to each other, "Here is the Señor doctor going to call on Doña Emilia. He has got his little coat on." The inference was true. Its deeper meaning was hidden from their simple intelligence. . . . The little white jacket was in reality a concession to Mrs. Gould's humanizing influence. The doctor, with his habit of sceptical, bitter speech, had no other means of showing his profound respect for the character of the woman who was known in the country as the English Señora.

The abandonment of the ragged native costume in which he had been liberated, in favour of clean clothes of European style indicates Monygham's desire to return, for Emilia's sake, to the world from which his past and his experience have cut him off.

The course of Monygham's career is not unlike Jim's. Both men are initially gifted and idealistically disposed, but both are trapped by circumstances into commission of a great betrayal, the guilt of which sets them apart from their own people. Just as Jim then compromises by taking the limited world of Patusan as the scene for the exercise of his talents, so Monygham, in order to practise medicine under Emilia's patronage, enters the faintly hostile social world of Sulaco, from which he has been long estranged. Each man enjoys the society of his heroine in his new environment, but each is threatened there by a rival (Cornelius and Gould respectively) who introduces a more serious and potentially fatal threat in the guise of a nemesis, a figure who confronts the hero with his past crimes.

Jim's nemesis is Brown who, on information supplied by Cornelius, is able to engineer the situation which results in Jim's defeat and death. Brown represents Jim's past failure to meet the standards of his own people and forces Jim into a reenactment of the *Patna* episode, into another betrayal of a group under his care, a betrayal which this time results in the hero's death. Monygham's nemesis is Señor Hirsch who, although in no way abetted by Gould, none the less comes to Sulaco to consult Gould and is first introduced to Monygham in Gould's drawing room. Monygham encounters Hirsch for the second time when he finds the dead, tortured body hanging from the beams of the upper room in the Custom House. Hirsch has been captured and tormented by Sotillo, who is determined to extort from him some story which will place the lost silver within his reach. In much the same way Monygham was himself years before tortured by one Father Berón for information about a nonexistent Costaguana conspiracy. On that occasion the doctor had "confessed," betraying his fellows and bringing upon himself a lasting sense of shame. In the hanging body of Hirsch, he is brought face to face with the nightmare that still haunts him.

Hirsch is the very personification of fear, the "man of fear," as Nostromo calls him, whose unsuspected presence in the lighter reveals to Sotillo the plot to remove the silver from Sulaco. There is, indeed, nothing more that Hirsch could have told Sotillo that the latter could not very quickly have deduced for himself, since the unfortunate prisoner had no idea of the treasure's real whereabouts. He belongs to no political party and subscribes to no particular ideal, but represents simply the human capacity for fear which, as Nostromo on the lighter with Hirsch is well aware, constitutes an unpredictable threat to any purposeful undertaking. " 'His being here is a miracle of fear—' Nostromo paused. 'There is no room for fear in this lighter,' he added through his teeth."

Monygham, like Jim, has in his past failed catastrophically to subdue his fear of hurt. His compromise consists in a superficial reconciliation with a society in which he has no faith, for the purpose of becoming once again a practising physician, a task which allows him to heal, or at least to ameliorate, the pains of others. His own pain, however, previously evaded by means of a false confession and betrayal, remains to be faced. In Hirsch Monygham is symbolically confronted with the fate he had once managed dishonourably to escape.

From this point the patterns of the careers of Jim and Monygham diverge, for whereas Jim fails to deal adequately with Brown and is consequently overcome, the doctor rises to the occasion symbolically presented by Hirsch and, rare among Conradian heroes, successfully expiates his old guilt. In the presence of Hirsch's body Monygham announces to Nostromo his plan, which consists, in effect, of a reenactment, in opposite moral circumstances, of his past crime. Formerly Monygham had been held prisoner by a political fanatic, tortured, and forced to betray others; now he proposes to place himself in the hands of Sotillo, another such fanatic, to risk torture and death by pretending to a secret knowledge of the whereabouts of the silver, and to make Sotillo think that he is willing to betray Gould and the pro-European party.

His object in all of this is to protect Emilia (and, coincidentally, the other Europeans and the mine workers) by causing Sotillo to think that the treasure is not lost but has been deliberately concealed by Gould. As long as Sotillo believes that the treasure may still be recovered, the doctor reasons, he will not waste time persecuting his political enemies. Yet Monygham, who himself believes the treasure lost in the Gulf and has no knowledge of its true location, clearly faces torture and death when Sotillo loses patience in the fruitless search.

In knowingly placing himself under such danger and in carrying out his plan to the last minute without wavering, the doctor does in fact achieve his purpose and save from Sotillo's vengeance Emilia and the other supporters of Gould's policies. Having long withstood Sotillo's threats, Monygham was on the very point of being hanged when the forces of rescue arrived. Having thus confronted and faced down the recrudescence of his past terror, he is free to enjoy his reward.

> "I've made my career—as you see," said the Inspector-General of State Hospitals [Monygham], taking up lightly the lapels of his superfine black coat. The doctor's self-respect, marked inwardly by the almost complete disappearance from his dreams of Father Berón, appeared visibly in what, by contrast with former carelessness, seemed an immoderate cult of personal appearance. Carried out within severe limits of form and colour, and in perpetual freshness, this change of apparel gave to Dr. Monygham an air at the same time professional and festive.

His expiation is marked by the departure of Father Berón, his old tormentor, from his thoughts, and his fuller acceptance into Emilia's circle is shown by his more deliberately formal style of dress. Moreover, with the increasing absorption of Gould in the affairs of the mine towards the end of the story Monygham finds his rival virtually removed from the field and himself in free possession of Emilia's companionship.

Monygham's bliss is not complete, of course, for he remains bitterly cynical in outward expression and is made miserable by Emilia's unhappiness. None the less Conrad leaves us in no doubt that the doctor is a happier man, rewarded both materially and spiritually for his final victory over fear. Very few other major Conradian figures are allowed to pass triumphantly through the cycle of failure, compromise, and nemesis. Why, then, is Monygham permitted to do so? The answer may be that Monygham is a special case, in that he is rendered, by his past experience, a man totally without illusion. Thereafter, much like MacWhirr (another triumphant hero, but one who is never guilty of moral failure), he becomes incapable of any great reach of imaginative self-deception such as leads the other heroes into untenable positions. His strength lies in that his view of the world is close to that of the author. Whether Conrad was himself as extremely prone to cynicism built upon a bedrock of sentimental sympathy is not quite the point; what is relevant is that the anonymous first narrator of *Nostromo* has a capacity for penetrating human pretensions and comprehending the feelings of others to a degree elsewhere approached in the story only in the character of Monygham. Intellectual perspicacity and human understanding are not qualities notably present in the usual Conradian hero; Heyst, the only other one who might claim to be significantly endowed with them, still falls behind Monygham in this respect. By means of these qualities Monygham arrives at a position of self-effacement and an estimation of the real value of human actions that makes him prepared to risk pain, death, and moral degradation, and in so doing to effect his own redemption.

At the same time Conrad portrays Monygham as a limited character, whose reward is circumscribed and whose success is not allowed to overshadow the falls, actual or imminent, of the surviving central figures of the story, Gould and Nostromo. The doctor remains a lonely and isolated figure, whose love for Emilia is not "the most splendid of illusions, but like an enlightening and priceless misfortune." His self-sacrifice for the good of the European community achieves its immediate end, but effects no lasting redemption beyond his own. Monygham is really no less cut off from the world around him at the conclusion of the story than he was at the beginning.

There remains Nostromo himself, the first of a new line of heroes, which also includes Verloc and Razumov. The earlier heroes, including Gould and Decoud, are placed in situations of self-defeating endeavour. They are men of unusual abilities which are generally directed outwards in attempts to improve the world along the lines of the heroes' ideals. They fail because flaws in their own natures render the ideals impossible of achievement without vitiating compromise. The new line of heroes, which begins here with Nostromo, presents us with a man whose object is no longer to pursue any ideal beyond the bounds of self-interest, but rather to attain the largely negative goal of surviving in passive comfort without compromising involvement in the conflicts of the world around him. Such men are Verloc, playing off anarchists against reactionaries for his own profit; and Razumov, seeking only to pursue his studies and lead a quiet life without political entanglements.

Such, too, is Nostromo, the first of the line, who appears in the same story as Gould, the last and perhaps the most magnificent of Conrad's idealistic supermen. The combination shows us that *Nostromo* is not only the second chronological turning point in Conrad's literary career but also a brilliant piece of structural composition creating between two characters a contrapuntal relation which forms the chief axis of the novel. Decoud and Monygham, important as they are, figure only episodically in the story, which turns upon the antithesis of Nostromo and Gould, "the two racially and socially contrasted men, both captured by the silver of the San Tomé mine." Gould is aristocratic, Anglo-Saxon, reserved and idealistic, while Nostromo is "a Man of the People," Italian, flamboyant and fundamentally self-centred. While Gould follows the established path of the early Conradian hero from idealism through compromise towards destruction, Nostromo, manifestly unidealistic and unconcerned with the state of the world at large, endeavours unsuccessfully to avoid precisely the kind of purposive action and moral commitment which is essential to Gould.

Nostromo, as he himself tells Decoud, has come to Costaguana "to make his fortune." Here he finds himself in a land of violent political tensions between two extremes, with both of which he develops loose affiliations. On the one hand he is a man of plebeian origin with deep roots in the common people, among whom he has a high reputation and a large following. On the other hand his wish to make his fortune, combined with his initial political neutrality, leads him to place his abilities at the disposal of the Sulaco oligarchy, represented by Captain Mitchell and ultimately by Gould himself. At the beginning of the events of the novel, therefore, Nostromo stands between the opposing forces of popular discontent and authoritarian government and is, moreover, a vital factor in the precarious balance between them; it is through his agency that the European party controls an effective work-force in Sulaco and keeps a semblance of order among the factions of the populace.

Giorgio and Teresa Viola are particularly important to the thematic structure of the story because they span the gulf between the Goulds' idealism and the popular movements by which Gould is opposed. The Violas, Giorgio as a former follower of Garibaldi and Teresa as a deeply religious woman and the story's mouthpiece of traditional demotic moral and domestic values, are at once of the people and at the same time committed to the highest of selfless goals, resolving what would otherwise remain a discord in the story between democracy and idealism. Giorgio Viola, "the Garibaldino," is an ardent republican who has fought for his cause both in Italy and South America. At the same time, however, he is "full of scorn for the populace, as your austere republican so often is," because, as himself a strict political idealist, he has no sympathy with the mercenary motives behind the popular movements in Costaguana. In this way he is naturally allied with both Charles Gould, as one who has striven after a vision of an improved world, and, as a democrat, with the people, including Nostromo. In a rather similar way Teresa is representative of basic moral and religious standards of personal integrity, which makes her at once the friend and protegée of Emilia and a strong-voiced advocate of proletarian values.

The Violas together represent a steady and uncompromising standard which contrasts, in the course of the story, with the respective moral disintegrations of both Nostromo and Gould. They succeed, in a sense, in preserving something of what both the chief heroes gradually lose. They do so, however, at considerable cost. They remain secondary and ineffective characters, variously protected or attacked by others but themselves initiating nothing. Teresa from the beginning suffers from an illness, a pain which, significantly, "had come to her first a few years after they had left Italy to emigrate to America and settle at last in Sulaco," and which finally kills her, not by mere coincidence, at the very moment when the town is taken over by revolutionaries. Giorgio survives, but becomes increasingly removed from the reality of things. From the beginning the inn which he keeps, named "Albergo d'Italia Una," signifies (so far as the story is concerned) an impossible dream, and towards the end Giorgio himself becomes a withdrawn, Bible-reading patriarch, whose ineffective attempts to apply traditional moral precepts to the upbringing of his daughters results in Nostromo's accidental death.

Nostromo's relations with the Violas reveal the tensions of his initial situation. On the one hand they are his adopted family, to whom he is both a son and something of a protector, and he has tacitly committed himself to eventually marrying their elder daughter, Linda. On the other hand, he has large personal ambitions which hinder him from settling into a life of hardworking orthodox domesticity, and in pursuit of these vague ends he labours for the rich European party, exerting himself to win the praise and attention of powerful men like Mitchell and Gould. Essentially Nostromo is seeking personal profit while avoiding commitment. The difficulties of this position are expressed in Teresa's criticisms of Nostromo's conduct. When we first hear her she is complaining that he has deserted the family in a time of danger in order to "run at the heels of his English." The fullest exchange between them takes place as she lies dying during the Monterist revolution.

> Nostromo said nothing, and the sick woman with an upward glance insisted. "Look, this one [the revolution] has killed me, while you were away fighting for what did not concern you, foolish man."
>
> "Why talk like this?" mumbled the Capataz between his teeth. "Will you never believe in my good sense? It concerns me to keep on being what I am: every day alike."
>
> "You never change, indeed," she said, bitterly. "Always thinking of yourself and taking your pay out in fine words from those who care nothing for you."
>
> There was between them an intimacy of antagonism as close in its way as the intimacy of accord and affection. He had not walked along the way of Teresa's expectations. It was she who had encouraged him to leave his ship, in the hope of securing a friend and defender for the girls.

As Teresa perceives, Nostromo's selfishness is holding him back from either making his fortune by commitment to the European party or settling into the regular life-pattern of the common people.

Nostromo keeps his options open by cultivating both the good opinion of his employers and popularity among the working classes. To commit himself to the democratic party or to adopt a normal plebeian level of existence would lose him the esteem of Mitchell and the Europeans, while to become an open supporter of the policies of Ribiera and Gould would deprive him of his popular support. Balanced between two worlds he occupies a unique position, on account of which he exercises considerable powers; his following among the people makes him an effective leader of the harbour work force, which in turn, as long as he steers clear of involvement in politics, makes him a valuable employee to Mitchell. Nostromo is thus the linchpin upon which the cohesion of local economy depends, the channel of command between the European capitalists and the local workers. Yet he can function in this way only as long as he avoids open espousal of either popular or patrician values, and as long as he holds aloof from both wealth and domestic obscurity.

Nostromo at the beginning of the story is living on his reputation, his popularity with the people, which makes him an effective leader, and his good name with the Europeans as an efficient foreman. His reputation depends upon his avoidance of commitment, and he is therefore an essentially vague character, without defined motives or long-range plans. The thin sketching of his personality in the first half of the story, far from being a weakness of the novel, is integral to its purpose. Nostromo, at the beginning, is indeed little more than a name. "The only thing he seems to care for, as far as I have been able to discover," observes Decoud, "is to be well spoken of." He is "a man for whom the value of life seems to consist in personal prestige." The number and variety of his names is in keeping with the nebulosity of his character. He is known variously as Nostromo, the Capataz, Gian' Battista, Juan, Giovanni and, later, Captain Fidanza.

The crisis of Nostromo's career comes when he accepts the job of removing the consignment of silver from Sulaco by sea in order to keep the Monterists from capturing it and, if possible, to deliver it to pro-separatist forces outside. This undertaking is not of his choosing, but is pressed upon him. To the Europeans he appears the only man for the job, and his vanity, when the matter is so put to him, causes him to accept it, yet Teresa sees at once the implicit dangers of the venture.

> "They have turned your head with their praises," gasped the sick woman. "They have been paying you with words. Your folly shall betray you into poverty, misery, and starvation. The very leperos shall laugh at you—the great Capataz."

After a little thought Nostromo begins to see that to take charge of the treasure is like "taking up a curse" upon himself, and that, without seeing quite what he was doing, he has given up the neutrality and good name which was the basis of his eminent position.

The point, as he soon realizes, is that for as long as he has charge of the treasure he is a marked man, whom anyone would kill to take it from him. The silver therefore exiles him. Once he has put out to sea with it he cannot come back; to return without it would be to admit publicly to failure or worse, and to return with it would be courting death. He sums up these conclusions in the lighter to Decoud.

> "Señor," he said, "we must catch the steamer at sea. We must keep out in the open looking for her till we have drunk all that has been put on board here. And if we miss her by some mischance, we must keep away from the land till we grow weak, and perhaps mad, and die, and drift dead, until one or another of the steamers of the Compania comes upon the boat with the two dead men who have saved the treasure. That, señor, is the only

way to save it; for, don't you see? for us to come to the land anywhere in a hundred miles along this coast with this silver in our possession is to run the naked breast against the point of a knife. This thing has been given to me like a deadly disease."

As Decoud perceives, Nostromo has "his own peculiar view of this enterprise."

His only course, having accepted charge of the treasure, is to deliver it as required to Barrios. Delivery of the treasure to Barrios, however, will virtually ensure the ultimate success of the separatists and, inevitably, make Nostromo one of the foremost heroes of their victory. From that point he will be largely identified with the governing party and will forfeit to that extent the following he has had among the people. Nostromo's acceptance of the job of delivering the silver occupies a point in his career exactly corresponding to the appearance of Haldin in Razumov's rooms and to the order Verloc receives to blow up the Observatory. From this moment the hero finds himself in the position of having to either take sides or go to the wall. He has, against his will, accepted compromise and commitment.

There follow the unforeseen collision with Sotillo's troopship and the concealment of the silver on the Great Isabel. When Nostromo returns he learns from Monygham that, through Hirsch, Sulaco now believes the silver to have been lost in the Gulf and Decoud drowned. At this point, other things being equal, Nostromo might simply have confided the real whereabouts of the treasure to Gould and returned to his normal duties. What deflects him from this path is his meeting with Monygham who, unintentionally, upsets Nostromo greatly by showing him how little the supposed loss of the treasure really means to the European party, who were concerned chiefly to remove it from the rebels' clutches. Nostromo begins to take the view that his own interests, and quite possibly his life, have been put at risk very lightly by people who now show no concern for the outcome of his adventure.

> "Was it for an unconsidered and foolish whim that they came to me, then?" he interrupted suddenly. "Had I not done enough for them to be of some account, *por Dios*? Is it that the *hombres finos*—the gentlemen—need not think as long as there is a man of the people ready to risk his body and soul? Or, perhaps, we have no souls—like dogs?"

In this frame of mind he returns to the home of the Violas to decide what he should do.

Teresa had died shortly after Nostromo's departure with the silver, killed by the sound of a shot fired by one of the rebels "as surely as if the bullet had struck her oppressed heart." Nostromo feels particularly guilty on this score, because he had refused to fetch her a priest, as she had requested, in order to keep his appointment with the lighter of silver. By the time he gets back to shore, disgusted at the dangers to which he has been so lightly exposed by the Europeans, he is strongly inclined to accept both Giorgio's republicanism and Teresa's advice. "They keep us and encourage us as if we were dogs born to fight and hunt for them," he says of the rich. "The vecchio [Giorgio] is right. . . . Teresa was right too."

At the inn after his return Nostromo meets Giorgio, who advises him, for purely idealistic reasons, to do as Monygham has suggested and depart at once by train with a vital message for Barrios. Nostromo does so, having no time to pass on to anyone he trusts (he does not trust Monygham) the truth about Decoud and the silver. When he returns to the scene some time later, events have taken the decision out of his hands. With Decoud dead and four bars of silver gone with him to the bottom of the Gulf, Nostromo cannot tell the truth without incurring suspicion of theft and even murder. Yet Nostromo, like Gould, having compromised and taken risks, appears to have been successful. He has made his fortune.

His success, however, like Gould's, plunges him into a network of typical Conradian ironies. Although he now possesses a far greater personal fortune than he can ever have hoped for, he can reap only fractional benefit from it for fear of discovery. On him, as on Gould, material wealth has a deleterious psychological effect. A man accustomed to living openly and rejoicing in popular acclaim, Nostromo now becomes furtive and cut off from those around him.

> And to become the slave of a treasure with full self-knowledge is an occurrence rare and mentally disturbing. But it was also in great part because of the difficulty of converting it into a form in which it could become available. . . . The crew of his own schooner were to be feared as if they had been spies upon their dreaded captain. He did not dare stay too long in port. . . . To do things by stealth humiliated him. And he suffered most from the concentration of his thoughts upon the treasure.
>
> A transgression, a crime entering a man's existence, eats it up like a malignant growth, consumes it like a fever. Nostromo had lost his peace; the genuineness of all his qualities was destroyed.

Once again Conrad uses dress to accentuate a change in the inner man. In his days of innocence Nostromo dressed naturally "in the checked shirt and red sash of a Mediterranean sailor," but after he obtains the treasure we see "the vigour and symmetry of his powerful limbs lost in the vulgarity of a brown tweed suit." The unsuitable clothing is the outward sign of the paradox of Nostromo's new situation as a rich man who must pretend relative poverty, a man of the people who must hide from public view, a sailor who dresses like a shopkeeper.

At a deeper level, however, Nostromo's situation remains much the same as it was. His object is still to "make his fortune," to use and enjoy the treasure which has now come into his possession. Against this object are the demands that he should enter into society, abandon his solitary, uncommitted way of life and undertake a proper measure of responsibility and public purpose. These demands, formerly voiced by Teresa Viola, are in the closing stages of the story represented by her elder daughter, Linda, the woman whom Nostromo is generally expected to marry. "Linda, with her mother's voice, had taken . . . her mother's place." Nostromo has no particular desire to marry Linda, for he is attracted to her younger sister, Giselle, yet he cannot marry Giselle, because Giorgio would not permit the elder daughter to be so passed over, and neither can Nostromo carry her off, for fear of losing the silver.

The connection between the Viola girls and the treasure is established when a lighthouse is built on the Great Isabel where Nostromo has concealed the silver. He secures the appointment of Giorgio as keeper of the light, knowing that he himself will then be able to visit the island publicly as Linda's suitor. The silver thus prevents him from offending Giorgio by either repudiating Linda or running off with Giselle. To continue his visits to the treasure he is obliged to accept open betrothal to the elder daughter.

The two girls represent the paradoxical tension between Nostromo's goal, the satisfaction of his appetites, and the gravitational pull of social norms. The orthodox Linda, like Teresa, stands for public and approved domestic stability, whereas Giselle is licentious, passionate and thoroughly desirable in a definitely unconventional fashion.

> As time went on, Nostromo discovered his preference for the younger of the two. . . . His wife would have to know his secret or else life would be impossible. He was attracted by Giselle, with her candid gaze and white throat, pliable, silent, fond of excitement under her quiet indolence; whereas Linda, with her intense, passionately pale face, energetic, all fire and words, touched with gloom and scorn, a chip off the old block, true daughter of the austere republican, but with Teresa's voice, inspired him with a deep-seated mistrust.

The treasure itself dictates that Nostromo should prefer Giselle, for he could not reveal its secret to the "austere" Linda, who has inherited her parents' high and idealistic standards. Giselle, who embodies his desire for freedom and luxury, is quite compatible with his possession of the silver and is even entrusted with knowledge of its existence. The irony lies in the fact that, precisely because of the treasure, Nostromo cannot make his preference for Giselle publicly known.

We can recognize here a familiar Conradian theme and pattern. In the tension between Nostromo's desires and what is generally expected of him we see the old opposition of selfish freedom and social responsibility, of licence and control, previously explored in the stories of Wait and Kurtz. Each of the Viola sisters stands at one pole of this dichotomy, Giselle symbolizing the hero's personal will and desire, Linda his moral duties in the public domain. They therefore take on the roles of heroine and anti-heroine respectively in relation to Nostromo. Giselle is the heroine, the woman who stands at the centre of the world the hero desires to enter. Linda is the anti-heroine, the rival for the hero's affections who comes from the orthodox world he has deserted through his compromise. It is no accident that Linda becomes keeper of the lamp "that would kindle a far-reaching light upon the only secret spot of his life."

The ending of Nostromo's story is worked out in terms of the familiar pattern employed earlier for Willems and Kurtz. In pursuing his personal goals the hero turns his back on the world of moral orthodoxy and commits a crime. The new life he wishes to shape for himself is directed towards a heroine, a young and desirable woman, but the hero is still tied to the anti-heroine, who belongs essentially to the respectable, authoritarian world he has abandoned. His position is threatened by a rival, who advances a competing claim to the heroine's affections, and he is finally confronted with fatal consequences by a male figure, the nemesis of an offended orthodoxy, who exacts punishment for the original

Nostromo's rival is a pale and insubstantial figure, put into the story, one suspects, merely to complete the pattern. This is Ramirez, who has succeeded Nostromo as captain of the Sulaco cargadors and who, like him, has fallen violently in love with Giselle. Ramirez watches Nostromo jealously, discovers his nightly visits to the island and, thinking that Giselle is the reason, reports these to Linda. Nostromo is not shot because of Ramirez' information, for Giorgio thinks he is shooting at Ramirez himself, but the threat of eventual discovery through the rival's jealousy is present in the story's closing pages.

The nemesis is Giorgio, an Italian of republican sympathies like Nostromo, but separated from him by a strict idealism which looks down upon material motives, an "austere contempt for all personal advantage." Giorgio, who "had all his life despised money," stands opposed to Nostromo, the thief of the silver. The albeit accidental shooting of Nostromo is therefore a retribution for the theft and for the motive of personal gain, which had all along prevented Nostromo's final entry into the Viola family.

The patterning of characters in the final phase of Nostromo's story is virtually identical to that in "Heart of Darkness" and therefore bears close similarity also to those of *An Outcast of the Islands* and (apart from the female figures) *The Nigger of the "Narcissus."* The situation may be represented in a diagram. . . .

	MALE	FEMALE
1st (ORTHODOX) WORLD	Nemesis (Giorgio)	Anti-heroine (Linda)
2nd (UNORTHODOX) WORLD	Rival (Ramirez)	Heroine (Giselle)

Here, as in ["Heart of Darkness"], the central theme is a contrast between duty and personal desires—respectively the first and second "worlds" of the diagram—with the nemesis figure and the anti-heroine belonging to the realm of the former and standing opposed to the rival and the heroine. Again strong personal animosities develop between the nemesis figure and the rival (Giorgio thinks he is shooting at Ramirez) and between the anti-heroine and the heroine (Linda knows Giselle is flirting with her betrothed and at one point attacks her physically).

We have seen that Nostromo first appears as a hero of a different kind from Kurtz. Kurtz is one of the line of Conradian central figures, running from Wait to Whalley and Gould, who are embodiments of paradox, and whose careers are therefore models of self-defeating endeavour. Nostromo is the first of those whose object is not to achieve a positive ideal but to secure their own comfortable independence in worlds of conflicting extremes. His immediate successors are Verloc and Razumov, both of whom wish only to steer noncommital courses of safety between warring parties. The outstanding problem is why Conrad reverted, for his conclusion of *Nostromo*, to the structural pattern of the earlier stories, introducing several new characters in order to do so (for both Linda and Giselle, as well as Ramirez, are effectively new in the last two chapters of the book), returning to the highly-charged symbolic manner of the tales of Wait and Kurtz.

The result suggests a possible degree of uncertainty in handling the new heroic style or, more probably, a wish to keep the novel from growing disproportionately long. *Nostromo* is the only novel in which Conrad attempted to deal simultaneously with a plurality of heroes, and their careers within it are not entirely coterminous. As Gould's affairs are approaching what promises to be a cataclysmic resolution, Nostromo is still setting out on his attempt to balance a compromise between opposing forces. His act in appropriating the silver corresponds structurally to Verloc's attempt on the Observatory and to Razumov's betrayal of Haldin, both deeds which take place relatively early in their respective stories. Had Nostromo been accorded a development of plot proportionate to those of his successors, it seems fair to assume that his story would have been prolonged to something like twice its present length. It may be that, foreseeing this, Conrad opted for a quick ending, to achieve which he drew upon the fictional mechanisms he had already evolved for dealing more rapidly with the heroes of shorter stories.

Silver and Silence: Dependent Currencies in *Nostromo*

Aaron Fogel

Nostromo is a smaller giant novel, an oxymoron of scale, and not simply a work of vast historical scope. Rhythmic obstacles—jerkinesses and breaks that interrupt the expansive prose—force the reader to share a feeling of historical disproportion with the characters, as well as tensions between force and farce. The novel establishes a rhythm of contraction against expansion. A historical understanding of this contradictory rhythm governing the sometimes vast and sometimes Lilliputian Sulaco can free us at least in part from Leavis's split evaluation of the novel as great but finally "hollow." His judgment anticipates many other strong but slightly unfair statements about Conrad as elusive, cold, stilted. These complaints are reasonable— anybody can see the source of them—but they come in part from a desire to set his work tonally inside the framework of the English "sympathetic" moral imagination and against the background of the great nineteenth-century historical novel. These standards don't apply, or aren't entirely applicable, because Conrad has an ironic relation to these traditions. Canonization has led to overemphasis of his historical range and blindness to his other side—his stubborn, even Menippean dislike of greatness. *Nostromo* isn't exactly meant to have the inclusive sympathetic force of *War and Peace*, *Bleak House*, *Middlemarch*, or even *Waverly*, but reads partly like an ironic attack on historical scope, a contracted scale model of "the great novel"— like the model ships Conrad encouraged his son John to build. His well-known comment, in the Note to *The Secret Agent*, that *Nostromo* had been his

From *Coercion to Speak: Conrad's Poetics of Dialogue.* © 1985 by the President and Fellows of Harvard College. Harvard University Press, 1985.

"largest canvas" stands more in relation to his own fiction than to that of other writers. His largest canvas may still be less grandiose than a historical novel by, for example, Henryk Sienkiewicz. The word *canvas* itself, beneath the obvious metaphor, may even connote sailing, the grandest sailing ship being small compared to a modern steamer.

Close reading will show that Conrad did not want to write a great national novel or even a great ironic provincial novel. Though Avrom Fleishman has accurately deflated what he calls "the Polish myth" about Conrad by sketching ethnic and social relations in the part of the Ukraine where he grew up, there is no doubt that Conrad saw himself as Polish. Where major works by Tolstoy, Melville, and Dickens, whatever their melancholy about scale, try to achieve a great rhythm appropriate to their great nations or cities, and where provincial novels enlarge small communities, Conrad insists on an a priori confusion about scale itself, paying attention to a large community that is at the same time small, half inside and half outside a "great world" that is somehow trivial. In *Nostromo*, paltriness and greatness often show up undecidably fused in the same person or incident. Nostromo's adventure on the lighter, for instance, is pettily grand. In the central political action, when Sulaco secedes, does secession amount to becoming larger or smaller? Is secession success? Is the newly condensed nation made practicably small (as Rousseau suggested Poland should contract to preserve freedom), or is it in fact only enslaved to a greater empire? Stylistically *Nostromo* mocks "greatness," and has a consistent strain of anti-imperial puns, dialogical fusions, and noise. It jeers at and violently contracts the scope of the great novel. Edward Said, one of the novel's most serious readers, takes up this question (for different reasons, since he argues that Conrad's motive for narrative disorder is to break with authorial intention), and writes about standard comparisons to *War and Peace*: "In sheer size, of course, the two novels are similar; but beyond that, comparing them is not valuable." Yet the two books are not similar in sheer size. He then goes on—as if looking for justification by another standard of immensity—to compare the book's epically clumsy quality to that of *Moby-Dick*. The comparison is strong, but again *Nostromo* has a much more skeptically confined idiom of space—sometimes like that on a chessboard—than Melville's epic.

Politically the main theme of *Nostromo* may be the impossibility of real secession—the forced dialogue of Sulaco with the outside world. Sulaco wins independence through separation, but this effects inclusion in a larger empire. The story of *Nostromo*, then, is partly that of the attempt of one smaller but vast "place"—not clearly defined as a nation or a province—to contract for autonomy within an expansionist setting. "If the country of

Poland was, curiously," Fernand Braudel writes of the sixteenth century, "a kind of free-trade area or rather an area of free passage with a minimum of duties or tolls, it was also a vast expanse, 'twice as big as France.'" As with historical Poland, we are left uncertain as to geographical and commercial status. The center of attention here is colonial dependency, in dialogue form, in imagery, and in spatialization. The snakes, the ropes and threads from which characters are suspended, the rocking chair on which Avellanos sits, the silences, the silver, the recurrent forced dialogues—images and relations are organized around the idea of forced dependency. And if we want to understand the dialogical force of *Nostromo*, both in its own form and in its relation to other writings, we have to point toward the special poetics of this ironic project, which led Conrad to reject, more than Scott, the historical novel's dialectic of inclusion, and to insist upon the falsity of any historical "dialectic" that disguises or ignores the reality of the coercive dialogic.

When Dickens begins *Bleak House*, the grim chime name "London," to make an understatement, locates the novel for his audience, and foretells the chiming prose to follow. Dickens, of course, doesn't have to supply a London map. Sulaco, by contrast, not unlike a place in Swift, is mapped for the reader in the first chapters: the shape of the harbor, the islands, the circum-scribing mountain chain or cordillera, the position of the mine, the alameda. But it is done so as to implicate the reader in a problem of scale. On the one hand it is alien, a very limited stage, as was the deck of the *Narcissus*; at the other extreme, and not only to avoid making this place too small or too much like a stage for reductive satire, Sulaco is also "vast" and almost equivalent to all of nature. This is a deliberate proportional anomaly in the opening chapters. Conrad builds us not a stage but what has to be called a problem geography, in the way that we speak of Shakespeare's "problem plays," making the reader work on a dilemma of scale. The geographical question of Sulaco—a country, a province, vast, small, part of Costaguana, part of the sea—is imposed at the outset on the reader by the opening descriptions long before Decoud's secessionist plan appears.

Lawrence Graver has argued that Conrad's "shorter fictions," the novellas or long stories, are his most perfect works, but that he tended to lose his way in his novels. Graver speaks of the "longer short" pieces as the most perfect. This thesis is right to consider scale the agony of Conrad's prose, but a little too simple. Aesthetic and political proportion are not for Conrad separable issues. In his image of the world, Russia is largeness, Poland relative smallness, Napoleonic Europe largeness, England a bleakly brilliant compromise, contract, or bargain, like his own life, between small-ness and largeness. A novella might be successful in aesthetic scale, and achieve aesthetic unity, but fail to take on real quandaries of scale in the political world: its perfection is its limitation. Conrad in fact deliberately writes novellas that go on too long and large novels which are somehow abrupt, and this is a kind of historical wit. In the Author's Note to *Nostromo* Conrad describes himself as returning to his family from obsessive work on the book "somewhat in the style of Captain Gulliver"—who was of course caught up in a bathos of scale, between megalomania and insignificance — and also gives the book a carnivalesque source in José Avellanos's never-published *Fifty Years of Misrule*. These burlesques of the book's in fact agonized production remind us that for all its immensity and seriousness, it has many stops and dwarfing ironies, offered with a good deal of Bakhtin's *rire resorbé* —hints of other more comic genres, and of what the narrator calls "mock solemnity"—and is indebted to Swift, perhaps even to Rabelais, for a sense of joking about its own proportions. Conrad's well-known preference for Turgenev over Dostoyevski and Tolstoi is partly a matter of scale.

Stealing Graver's phrase to travesty it, then, we could say that even *Nostromo* is one of Conrad's "shorter fictions." Graver may be right that Conrad worked best scaling down, but he fails to see how this happens most effectively and absorbingly not in the novellas, where compression is formally typical, but in his political novels, *Nostromo*, *The Secret Agent*, and *Under Western Eyes*, all three of which put the scope of larger historical novels under an idiosyncratic and surprising contractual pressure. Some of this pressure, I will try to show, appears in the Menippean device of organizing its own information as the result of "forced dialogue." That is, pressing people to speak, inquisitorial process, yields a kind of truth, whose origin itself is in question. The result of this process, which shows the prose that we read as "forced" in its forcefulness, is a contraction of Romantic prose energy. "Expansion" and "contraction," which are the problems of imperialism, are also the problems of prose form in historical narration. This conflict is simultaneously political (having to do with the reining in of the expansive rhetoric of imperialism), aesthetic (having to do with the dramatic relation of prose masses to each other as presented to the reader), and dialogical (having to do with the amount each person speaks in a dialogue).

Nostromo is in fact a dialogue with a number of energetic works usually not mentioned. Cunninghame Graham's *Mogreb-el-Acksa*, with its picture of a "sub-European" Morocco in which Muslims, Jews, and Christians are brought together into continual uneasy contact, and its mobile, traveling sentences, had a complex influence on Conrad in this period—though partly because he quarreled with its simple linguistic flamboyance and the nature of its assumptions about polyglossia. The "Italian" element in *Nostromo*—the

Garibaldian politics and melodramatically "operatic" pitch—recalls the more general use of Italian settings in English tradition, from Shakespeare to Browning, to mean anarchic, Machiavellian, and therefore dramatically interesting politics, but of a kind that doesn't hit satirically home. The strongest and most similar text among all *Nostromo*'s ancestors may be *The Peloponesian Wars*, and not the later histories which Conrad used for documentation. Conrad arguably had wide classical reading, and the counterpoint in *Nostromo* between dense realpolitik and scenes of ironically framed set speeches resembles Thucydides' version of the classical irony about speech and action. Thucydides' most famous problem scene is itself a colonial "forced dialogue," the Dialogue at Melos. *Nostromo* recalls Thucydides also in its intricate and demanding sentence style based on phrasal verbs; and in its historical context, that of a colonial world of "force" and dismal dependency, in which political speech conceals its unfreedom by rhetorical flourish. Finally, what *Nostromo* may owe to Swift is that prose masses on the page sometimes appear in visibly excessive, even scatological *dis*proportion, as a part of the satirical and political meaning. Even if we exclude the element of popular romance full of various "types" who will capture an audience, *Nostromo* has an intention which is at least double: first as a realistic, even vast, history, but second as an ingenious satiric "miniature" of the disproportions in relations that occur under imperialism. This complex intention must be held together, but *not* "unified," by a general sense of forced relation. As in the other political novels, Conrad here seems to burlesque his own unusual powers of international synthesis. He does not mean, as does Pound in the *Cantos*, to bring international variety into a unity of civilized feeling. On the contrary, he shows us, intentionally, a variegate hodgepodge, held together only by his own openly arbitrary force as a novelist, as the characters also force each other into relation.

A first sense of force as disproportion appears in the portrait of the banker Holroyd—the first figure in *Nostromo* whose speech as proportion receives specific comment. He believes expansively that he can hold the world together as one coherent empire. Holroyd's personal rhythms express the historical period *Nostromo* seeks to capture. The key word for him would be *filibuster*; though Conrad does not himself use the word, Cunninghame Graham does, again in *Mogreb-el-Acksa*, to refer to his own reputation as a rover, and Conrad later calls Peyrol a "freebooter," from which the more cynical and politically shady modern term derives. The word *freebooter*, which also appears in Scott, applies, though at a historical slant, to a whole class of Conradian post-Romantic heroes, from Lingard to Whalley to Nostromo to Peyrol. In each case, however, the story shows how specific historical or political "tethers" bind and contract the figure of the freebooter, so that this type of Conradian hero is another trope of coercion, the "unfree freebooter," whose gift for roving and "free piracy" is now politically under "contract." Politicized freebooting is "filibuster." The "unfree freebooter" in Conrad—the filibuster or hired man of force —acts in the field of coercive contractual politics and usually fails in some way. Nostromo himself is this figure on a ledge between the two conditions.

But *filibuster* as a dual and historically dialogized term—like *impression* —is a good metaphor for the entire novel *Nostromo* because it also links disproportion in action to disproportion in oratory. These are, the novel shows, parallel problems in a colonial setting. We should remember that as a noun *filibuster* means, first of all, "an American who in the mid-nineteenth century took part in fomenting revolutions and insurrections in a Latin-American country"; nineteenth-century slang only secondarily and figurally makes it the pirating of parliamentary time by a minority or dependent group. By bringing up this word, which Conrad does not use —as by bringing up Graham, Thucydides, and Swift—I am trying to reinforce our sense of the age in which Conrad and his readers felt immersed, and which he was both criticizing and representing, when he created his own narrative methods of plural filibuster. As speech, filibuster is a kind of morosely politicized sailor's yarn; the Spanish idiom *hablar de la mar* means "endless speech." A filibuster, as a personal noun, is a politicized freebooter; but as a parliamentary speech act it resembles that "temporizing," stalling, monologuing delay which has always been recognized as a key to Conrad's narrative technique, yet which has never been fully grasped as a political, as well as poetic, rhythm.

The genius of *Nostromo* in its prose rhythms is to render the emergence of filibuster as both action and speech on all sides of the colonial relation: those in power and those who are powerless all filibuster. The San Franciscan, Holroyd, for example, foments his own Latin American revolution by directive investment; visiting Gould he talks in egotistical, expansive monologues—seen on the page —about his expansionist religion in a way that Gould rejects but can't openly criticize. The representation of talkative people is an old comic device, but here we have something different from Austen's Miss Bates or Scott's pedants. The equation made on the page is clear: his talk expands to take over as his politics does. By contrast and resemblance, many other characters indigenous to Sulaco, and weaker, filibuster more secretly and pathetically, insofar as each is forced to work at his own incongruous revolution, and to make his own monologue about it. Certainly the ancestor of José Avellanos might be found in Walter Scott's

loquacious old Scotsman, whose lengthy jargon, sometimes nearly unread-
able, often indicates the historical pathos of speaking at length in a "dead"
language, and who talks so much because he is a living encyclopedia of a
group about to disappear. But Conrad's gesture, though it grows out of this
tradition, seems more abstract and planned: the historical period which *Nostromo* seeks to give us via prose rhythm is one in which Romantic expansive
"freebooting" has turned into "filibustering," both in action and in speech—
that is, in which the Romantic piratical free agent, and the expansively
hopeful monologuing self, are in process of losing their glamour, and have
come under contraction and contract. Parliamentary coherence in aggressive
debate threatens to degenerate into a "concatenation" (Eloise Knapp Hay's
word) of pathetically forceful monologues. Romantic poetry, expansive about
the joyous self, now seems a function of expansionism in politics. Romanticism is expansionism: that was the pivot of Marlow's self-recognition. In this
context, if there were no forced dialogue to hold speech together, speech in
Nostromo would be only anarchic pathos. Instead, "masses of words" are
dramatized as imperial, not Romantically free, energies.

To read *Nostromo*, then, is to have our idea of the "field" of dialogue,
in both politics and aesthetics, forcibly changed, and to move out of a world
of parliamentary dialogue into one of general filibuster. In both its meanings,
the dialogical world of "filibuster" opposes, or subverts, the liberal parliamentary idea that energetic public speech, for all its conflict and egoism, can
cohere positively, and lead to collective action. Parliaments work in nations,
not for empires or colonies. "A lot of words" here is often synonymous not
with parliamentary spirit but with hopelessness and the inability to be heard.
Individuals act diversely to foment each his own revolution in the Americas;
dilatory, powerless talk has become the self-caricaturing *essence* of an ineffective parliament. Decoud's skepticism may often be a pose, but there is
no doubt that his ridicule of Parliament as a *Gran' bestia* is partly endorsed. In
the true parliamentary idea of dialogue—to be found from Milton to early
Dickens at the core of "English" energy—everyone heatedly but addres-
sively tries to exert as much power over public dialogue as he can. Dickens
caught this brilliantly in what are in some sense the "first" pages of his
work, the description of the mutual insults of the Pickwick Club, which
hilariously transform themselves into praise. There may be shouting down,
interference, and denunciation, but even at its most brutal and dilatory the
parliamentary image optimistically implies some communal action, and the
assumption by all the speakers that they address someone and belong. "Filibuster" appears because parliamentary form collapses under the weight of
imperialist and colonial disproportions. The technique of filibuster was first

used in the British parliament as the strategy of the nearest colony, Ireland (think of Swift again and *A Tale of a Tub*), and in the United States the filibuster is of course the exemplary speech act of the defeated South. Personal filibuster might be one way to describe the great power of Faulkner's style in *Absalom! Absalom!* and other works. The pathos of filibuster begins as a conscious tactical subversion of the dialogue of parliament—which implies that everyone belongs—by overdoing the right to be heard to the point where the principle annihilates itself. Instead of leaving the scene, the outnumbered minority speaker, to protest a lack of actual power, gains a futile, temporary "grieving" monopoly on talk which in no way hides his powerlessness in reality or his marginality in history. Filibuster then appears as a grievance against parliamentary order itself. This creates a new image of dialogue and speech in the novel. Faulkner's liking for Conrad can be traced partly to their shared intuition of the emergence of filibuster to replace the Dickensian exuberance of the parliament. The more language the speaker produces (including the writers themselves) the more they seem defeated, "taken over" by the force of history, dependent, Faulkner as Southern, Conrad as Polish.

Nostromo tries to capture this paradoxical rhythm of colonial talk in a prose of self-defeating rhythms. Verbal "expansion" and accumulation lack expansive Romantic joy. This is one reason for the book's unpopularity in spite of its virtuoso cast of Romantic characters, clearly a bid to attract an audience: Conrad here makes the very technique of Romantic expansiveness which he seems to be practicing deliberately joyless. This contracted expansiveness in prose style may be typical of a certain kind of poetic novel, in which condensation is ill at ease with narrative momentum. But here it "refers" rhythmically to the historical problem of expansion itself. As in the difficult prose rhythm, in politics neither contraction nor expansion is shown to be the simple answer.

As often in Conrad's best work, the alert characters are painfully conscious of the problems of speech proportion and discuss them openly, but are unable to alter them. The Goulds, for example, confront together the fact that both Holroyd and Avellanos talk a lot, and find themselves suddenly disagreeing:

> They had stopped near the cage. The parrot, catching the sound of a word belonging to his vocabulary, was moved to interfere. Parrots are very human.
>
> "Viva Costaguana!" he shrieked, with intense self-assertion, and, instantly ruffling up his feathers, assumed an air of puffed-up somnolence behind the glittering wires.

"And do you believe that, Charley?" Mrs. Gould asked. "This seems to me most awful materialism, and—"

"My dear, it's nothing to me," interrupted her husband, in a reasonable tone. "I make use of what I see. What's it to me whether his talk is the voice of destiny or simply a bit of claptrap eloquence? There's a good deal of eloquence of one sort or another produced in both Americas. The air of the New World seems favourable to the art of declamation. Have you forgotten how dear Avellanos can hold forth for hours here—?"

"Oh, but that's different," protested Mrs. Gould, almost shocked. The allusion was not to the point. Don José was a dear good man, who talked very well, and was enthusiastic about the greatness of the San Tomé mine. "How can you compare them, Charles?" she exclaimed, reproachfully. "He has suffered—and yet he hopes."

The working competence of men—which she never questioned—was very surprising to Mrs. Gould, because upon so many obvious issues they showed themselves strangely muddle-headed.

Charles Gould, with a careworn calmness which secured for him at once his wife's anxious sympathy, assured her that he was not comparing.

Here the Goulds between them divide up the meaning of those masses of words that challenge the reader's sense of rhythm on encountering the difficult opening movement of the novel. What are we to think of the production of "major force" by cumulative language? Is this force aesthetic or political? Is it force or farce? Is Avellanos's force the same as Holroyd's, or ethically different? Before siding too quickly with one of the speakers, we should recognize the intended dialogism: the equal case made for each side. The scene itself is framed and emblematized by the deceptively banal parrot, who screams out (in translation), "Long live the coast of bird-droppings," one instance of Swiftian satire partly hidden from the English audience by polyglossia. The slogan that comes out of a bird's mouth—its *bêtise*—will celebrate whatever comes out of its rectum or "mine." That is, the parrot is an emblem of ideological speech itself. The name Costaguana is typical of Conrad's punning—onomastic jokes being themselves allegorical coercions which the reader with an urge for freedom will usually want to resist. But that is the point: the parrot is not just the emblem of mechanically produced speech but a representative of language as not free but materially "caused." This is what Charles, the materialist, believes. Language is matter, and a lot coming from one mouth is the same as a lot coming from another. Language must be judged as pure extension, even as mass. Emilia, for once "almost shocked" by an idea of Charles's, insists on a self-evident ethical distinction between the two men: the wordy constitutionalist Avellanos articulates a social ethic that cannot be equated by plain word count to claptrap like Holroyd's material evangelism. But while obviously her critical idealism pervades the entire novel, she is not coextensive with its dramatic meaning. When Charles as a producer sees words only as mass and extension, he resembles Conrad's own working conditions, as a producer of many words for a living, more than does Emilia.

These two positions regarding amassed language —the ethical, which holds that the altruistic content of verbal expansiveness can be real, and the materialist, which dismisses all expansiveness as the same sublimation of imperial force in "inconclusive" prose rhythms—are irreconcilable and at the heart of the novel's tortured prose, of Conrad's quarrel with cumulative effect in the historical novel, and even with his own evolved techniques of *progression d'effet*, as described a little too preciously by Ford. Conrad often criticizes or mocks his own techniques for creating aesthetic "force." So the reader is meant to feel the amassing of prose in this novel itself, not simply as sublime energy, and not simply as historical "shit" (or excrementitious burden), but as the conflict between these. The prose-poetic question that the novel poses is: how are we to feel about the accumulation of language in any "great" historical or social novel whose physical mass as a big book is a weighty metaphor for populousness, even a demographic gesture? Is it potentially "beautiful," ethically high and sublime, socially inclusive, like a great constitution, potentially democratic and compassionate, as to Emilia and José; or is it always, even more violently than in the bleakness of late Dickens, some unconscious brand of "nationalist shit," the sublimated image of national greatness in the great massive novel? Thus when we scan *Nostromo* visually, or its amassed long paragraphs, and recall its temporal rhythms, we are presented with a question regarding massiveness itself.

Prose as the laborious production of masses of words is a recurrent theme in Conrad's letters, in which he often counts words in units of ten thousand, parentally scolding or praising himself for the month's yield. The parrot may come from Flaubert on banality, or may recall Melville's despair at writing as scrivening in his forced dialogue *Bartleby*—but it is also just a crude joke. Conrad's picture of himself as being compelled to write a lot, and his ability to register this strain and make it a prose rhythm, combine with his complex Polish sense of scale, and his very harsh sense of humor, to redefine the rhythmic ambition of the historical novel. To ignore his sadly "solemn mockery" of the ethical figures in the novel—even Emilia Gould, when she attends a birth of warm, fecal silver from the mine—is to sentimentalize his real case for them as persons with hopeful ideas. Leavis and Berthoud, who write brilliantly about the book in the tradition of moral criticism, nevertheless are a little too oblique or silent about this grosser laughter that has a different impact from high "irony." Consider this description of José Avellanos talking: "Then giving up the empty cup into his young friend's hand, extended with a smile, he continued to expatiate upon the patriotic nature of the San Tomé mine for the simple pleasure of talking fluently, it seemed, while his reclining body jerked backwards and forwards in a rocking-chair of the sort imported from the United States." This sentence imports the jerky physics of the rocking chair into its own syntax and shrieking rhymes in order to comment on Avellanos's dependent politics. The rhythmic form mocks the stated theme of fluency. The four *at*'s (expatiate, patriotic, nature) at the outset are monotonous, mechanical; the "it seemed" interrupts at just the wrong moment, after "fluently," for an effect of gross rhythmic farce; the image of the talking body of Avellanos sitting on a jerky machine indicates that he remains unconscious of the material base of his own eloquence; rest, unrest, arrest come together in false unison in the key motion of jerking; and the rocking-chair rhythm of the phrase "sort exported" shows us that Avellanos has an imported rhythm (rocking chairs being at this time a piece of furniture particularly associated with New England): his own rhetorical continuity and force are dependent. This is not to say that Conrad regards all parliamentary talk as just "superstructure"; but he does present most historical and political discourse as "jerkily" disconnected from historical reality. This "jerking" rhythm, with affectionate, almost Homeric satire about the tremors of the old, is associated throughout the novel with the speech and movements of Mitchell, Monygham, and Giorgio; it signifies both their broken physical courage and their various incomplete relations to the forced dialogues of social history. Avellanos, no matter how admirable in having survived torture, is a leisure-class figure in a rocking chair, somewhat cut off from material and social reality, whose speech, like the parrot's, derives from his "bottom," base, or seat.

Among other things, what Avellanos, like Mitchell, omits in his jerkiness is that labor is impressed, forced to work, imported, even enslaved. Impressment at the docks is left to Nostromo; he impresses laborers visually by his silver displays, and acts as a one-man press gang toward them, beating them to make them work. Such impressive "force" makes labor continuous. In discussing the "patriotic nature" of the mine, Avellanos also omits—as immediately afterward we are told Mrs. Gould knows—that "whole tribes of Indians had perished in the exploitation." Again, in this view of its supposed "nature," he omits the great joke, that Charles Gould himself owns the mine because it was originally *forced* on his father at a time when it was nonproductive; the mine itself has its origins in a grimly funny forced dialogue between the state and the Gould family. In all this the point is that Avellanos uses an unconscious oxymoron when he refers to "patriotic nature," just as Holroyd does more blatantly when he refers to the coming time for "proper interference" by North America in Sulaco. For Avellanos, the "deliciousness" of the rhetorical figure "patriotic nature" lies not only in its euphony but in its sublime combination of father and mother, patriotism and nature. But this is meant here to be an irrational synthesis: mines do not have patriotic natures, as interference cannot be proper, since it violates identity. Speaking about property and nature, the two fall into similar contradictions. The argument that Conrad had a bad ear for English, and was himself trying to capture euphoniously the rhythms of the rocking chair, would, I think, be nonsense. His sense of the English verb is acute; *jerk* is the key verb for going on without achieved continuity throughout the novel. At the very least, the contrast between Avellanos's alleged fluency and the rhythms of the imported chair gives some credence to Charles's materialistic reduction of him. At the most, it implies that Avellanos, however sympathetic, is as much of a historical fool, out of touch with the real "continuity and force" of history, and of class relations, as is the more obviously ludicrous historian Mitchell. Avellanos is materially dependent on the United States for his rhythms; his speech is jerky because dependent systems of thought are by nature full of gaps.

To summarize what has to be a set of indicators rather than a complete description of this part of the novel's prose poetic: (1) *Nostromo* is a small big novel because its play with scale calls into question the spirit of amassing which it creates. It continually "contracts" the noisiness and expansiveness it also renders. (2) It can be helpful to understand the organization of the whole novel, as history and as the aesthetics of dialogue, by the term *filibuster*. The multiple dependent speakers threaten the parliamentary image of collective speech as much as the multiple fomenters of different revolutions in action in Latin America. (3) The issues of amassed prose and of proportion in dialogue are inextricably fused as both aesthetic and political in Conrad's work.

One main unstudied question about the poetics of *Nostromo* deserves close attention: the chime between the economy of "silver" in the narrative and the economy of "silence" in the dialogues. In a singularly precise way . . . the whole of *Nostromo* works to demonstrate that the two economies run parallel in any society, and that in this particular one "silence is silver," not golden. Silence, the reserve of dialogical power, resembles silver, the reserve of political power, and both appear, when looked at closely, to be dependent, secondary currencies. They fluctuate in value in response to other currencies. Silver, for all its sometimes overworked visual recurrence in the book, has been carefully chosen by Conrad to displace gold as the "typical symbol" of value because it is less stable, and more dependent. In addition, as the lesser of the two "major" currencies, the smaller standard of value, silver had various meanings in the Americas at the turn of the century, and also, as we will see in a moment, makes a possible symbolic reference to Poland as a dependent nation. Silences likewise (at least the local silences in human dialogue, if not the natural silence of places like the Golfo Placido) are the lesser and more fluctuating part of social language; though sometimes silence in Conrad seems to be at the base of all dialogue, a reserve from which meaning is drawn, at least as often it seems by contrast dependent on and determined by the speeches surrounding it. He does not have a theory but a practice: his ability to exploit both these possibilities leads to much of the dramatic complexity of his writing. Throughout *Nostromo*, silver and silence become the linked defensive "possessions" of the various characters. The two elements are more meaningful together than alone: they indicate ironically that dependent persons who try to achieve autonomy have to do so through dependent, not absolute, means. This may be the most original feature of *Nostromo*, an extraordinary idea of linkage between the political economy and the dialogue economy that colonial people are forced to practice, formally registered by a polyphony between the dialogical and narrative forms of the novel. But to follow this prose chime—even to convince the reader that it is forcibly there—I will have to backtrack and discuss the way in which words are offered in the novel.

The geographical Sulaco, defended from the profane outside world, appears at the start as a natural temple of silence. The narrative, however, quickly dissolves this legendary, "dumb show" atmosphere (including the story of the gringos' silent death) to give a portrait of the progressive modernization of the country as "noise"—much as Decoud will later suggest, annoying Avellanos and Antonia by his own loud insistence, that colonial history is a progress of increasing noise. Though the opening folk tale about gringos and their ghostly fate has often been taken to foreshadow the action, it is also one of those legends frequently found in Conrad, whose silent simplicity is at odds with novelistic realism. The dumb show is a legend of silence; the novel is a history of both silence and noise. Especially during the riot, part 1 sets up a contrast between nature as silence and history as noise.

Between the absolute silence of the Golfo Placido and the total noise of anarchic riot, however, there is also music, which is here a kind of forced, or "strung-up," order, and characters here are implicitly orchestrated as different political instruments. Mrs. Viola, for example, takes her name from her sonorous, perhaps pseudoprophetic "contralto," which has an ambiguous effect on Nostromo's future; and less clearly, Decoud's name suggests "unstrung" or "unthreaded," so that it is, as will be clear further on, part of an entire system of "musical bondage" and the political instrumentalization of persons—derived from the forcible tuning of strings—in the imagery.

For an understanding of the use of words, names, and noises, however, the companion book to the first part of *Nostromo* is probably again Cunninghame Graham's *Mogreb-el-Acksa*. That book is sprinkled with foreign words, and has a random exuberance of polyglossia or languages in contact. Graham presents himself as an ethnographer of speech, a collector of folk proverbs, and a *bête noire* to his contemporaries, reversing their moralisms into antimoralisms of his own. In his witty protests he seems full of himself, where Conrad often seems, in direct contrast, empty of himself. As a result, what seems to be the common ground between them—ironic, detached criticism of a polyglot imperial world—is in fact the radical difference, because Graham finds it to be full, Conrad empty. Graham, for example, gives a waggish portrait of a vagabond as someone who "spoke almost every language in the world" and was therefore a "knave." Thus he seems to be debunking polyglossia. But at the same time Graham lets us know that he himself is the knave, the vagabond trickster, filling his book with clever insights. The book is filled with Spanish proverbs, jokes about the pretensions of philologists, and the entertainment of the mixed races of Morocco. Graham speaks in these heavily witty tones about naming: "How much there is in names; fancy a deity, accustomed to be prayed to as Allah by Arabs, suddenly addressed by an Armenian as Es Stuatz, it would be almost pitiable enough to make him turn an atheist upon himself." (The artfully assumed run-on speaking character of this syntax typified Graham's mobile style in the whole book.) "I feel convinced a rose by any other name does not smell sweet; and the word Allah is responsible for much of the reverence and the faith of those who worship him." He jokes, but he believes in the fullness of names. In spite of his apparent mockery of name superstition, as a stylist he creates a roving, rich, and exotic text full of interesting words and scenes. The book is a true travelogue.

Nostromo at first looks similar to *Mogreb-el-Acksa*. It presents us an American nation positioned roughly where Morocco is vis-à-vis Europe— "below"—and likewise "filled" with plural races. We get a medley of

Italian, English, Spanish, American, American Indian, and Jewish figures. One impulse Conrad had in constructing the book was no doubt to fill it with these so that it would sell. The modern reader who sees Conrad as gloomy forgets to what extent the work had to be sold as full of swashbucklers and dark women. But of course at the same time he does subvert his own romance with bitterness and skepticism, and gives, unlike Graham, a feeling of contraction. The names that speckle his text in various languages are mostly empty, lacking in appropriateness, in property. They are not Romantic but contractual, deliberately hollow, and often oxymoronic. Mrs. Viola, with her operatic faith in the force of speech, scoffs at Nostromo that his name is only a fool's contract: "He would take a name that is properly no word from them." But Nostromo's name, "taken from them," is a contract much like "Joseph Conrad," a contraction, and the word *proper* resonates emptily throughout the novel, most bitterly when Holroyd says his oxymoron, already quoted, about "the time for proper interference on our part." The littlest and ugliest of the islands is improperly named Hermosa— "beautiful"; the Rio Seco is the obvious oxymoronic place for Montero's great victory; the ubiquitous military guards are "serenos." From the beginning, steamship names from the Roman pantheon are inappropriate: "The *Juno* was known only for her comfortable cabin amidships, the *Saturn* for the geniality of her captain," and so on. What interests Conrad here is not the old boy's lament that words are losing their meaning. Conrad has a much larger intelligence of the transience of language and names in history. Though there is an obvious joke in the discrepancy between the Roman gods' attributes and the individual boats and captains, Rome *itself* is appropriate to this context of modern imperial sailing. What interests him is that figures like Mrs. Viola, who believe "profoundly" in the individual propriety of names miss the larger force and continuity within changing language and history. A name that is improper for the individual, and that lacks appropriateness to his first character or being, may by that very emptiness be true to the force of history. "Nostromo," the name as renamed, as renown (compare the French *renommé*) is "taken from them" because fame necessarily has the structure of being renamed for others. Józef Korzeniowski himself altered his name so that it would have English currency. There is accurate comedy in the fact that the new *Saturn* is known for geniality. The fact that the original tones of names are "detonated" or "unthreaded" by history does not fill Conrad with conservative horror, or with the desire, like Graham, to be a wag. Names of historical persons *are* contracts. Mrs. Viola has a case when she points out that Nostromo is paid in words but is not even allowed his own name; but the fact that it is someone named Mrs.

Viola who says this should lead us to suspect the sonority of the criticism as much as anything else.

Just as Decoud hears history in the changing noises of Sulaco, the reader is meant to hear the many little noises, splutters, and renamings in the prose, and to organize them skeptically as signs of colonial history. Though it is risky to posit a "global" sense of names and words, it would be helpful to emphasize the frequent contractual emptiness of naming here. This is a kind of polyphony which is not "fullness" and not historical or social "plenitude." In Bakhtin's concept of novelistic diction as "heteroglossia" or "polyglossia" (plurality of dialects, languages, and ideologies), the novel in its truest generic examples shows forth the irreconcilable languages of different groups—classes, nationalities, and professions. These give the novel its unique sense of plenitude as surfeit, and its special powers to present a variety of consciousnesses. Bakhtin's work is great; yet the crude criticism could be leveled that, in spite of his desire to affirm "otherness," his work adds up, surprisingly enough, to an encomium on expansive nationalism. The novel, in all its exuberance, equals the various, large, cacophonous, tolerant, multivoiced nation—and the favorite examples will be national geniuses like Dickens and Dostoyevski—whose robust dialogics Bakhtin advocated partly as a protest against his own political situation. The relation of *Nostromo* to this pluralism of the historical novel is unusual to the point of being bizarrely antithetical. Conrad equally apprehends, but does not equally celebrate, what Bakhtin sees. The "heteroglossia" here, the polyphony of ideas, the diverse, irreconcilable languages have no exuberant flavor. Conrad imagined a more forced and negative "polyglossia," not exactly Babel, but a world in which the plurality of languages and ideas does not amount to a new plenitude. It only exists, marked by ironies, emptinesses, contractions, and contractualities of its own, rather than by glorious worldliness and freedom. That is, Conrad created, from his Polish-English contractual standpoint, a deliberately hollow and coercive international polyphony.

It is in this strangely ironic, oxymoronic, contractual, historically emptying context of naming in *Nostromo* that we have to ask the question, Why is the Gould mine a silver mine? Why choose silver as the ore and then name the owning family Gould? The false easy answers are two. One is that gold and silver are functionally identical here; the Gould family name indicates its position as source of value in Sulaco. The contrary, slightly less oversimplified reading would argue that this naming is a harsh oxymoron, almost on the order of Orwellian satire, which points mockingly to the relative instability and worthlessness of the novel's actual fetish of silver, as opposed to the family's illusory idealism in its search for a stable and perfect standard of value and of politics for Costaguana.

Neither reading is precise. Instead, silver in the novel has to be understood both in its relation to the book's dialogue forms and in its historical connotations. *Heart of Darkness*, as we saw [elsewhere], "chimed" Ivory to Invoice, the economic standard of value to Marlow's obsession with an "invoice," a powerful, idealist, standard-giving Kurtz. In that story the two fetishes equally required critique, but Marlow's effort to liberate himself from his idea of Kurtz's voice was a more difficult and prolonged "secondary" struggle, ending in the realization that forced dialogue, not freedom, is the form of Intention. *Nostromo* carries on, but in a more subtle and unforgettable way, this project of a chiming or parallelism between an economic currency—in Sulaco silver—and an illusory, pseudoliberating dialogical currency—in Sulaco no longer voice but silence. As often in Conrad, the alteration of a commonplace, as if both to rivet and revise the thinking of a large audience, is being undertaken without Flaubert's contempt or hilarity. According to convention, of course, "silence is golden." In the structure of *Nostromo*, "silence is silver." That is, both are secondary or dependent currencies, relatively unstable in comparison to the main currencies, language and gold.

Put the poetics of the parallelism between silence and silver aside for a moment, and consider the historical theme of silver. In the Americas at the time Conrad describes, bimetallism was a major popular issue; silver symbolized the increased distribution of wealth downward without forsaking the standards of capitalism. In the *Titanic* essays eight years later Conrad refers ironically to "nasty, cheap silver," parodying the voice of the superrich who might have to use it on a sea journey. One need not connect Charles Gould to William Jennings Bryan to see that Gould uses the idea of "cheap" silver as the more democratic and politicized of the two standards of value to half convince Emilia that his is an idealist capitalism, ultimately good for "the people." Silver will spread the wealth; when it is appropriated by Nostromo, the man of the people, as a secret hoard to which he is also in some sense entitled (actively and in dialogue, because no one has asked him about it), the political connotations are intentional: Nostromo has taken by covert silent force a form of popular wealth that was patronizingly given him before. And just as silver has a dependent but varying relation to gold— a restless relation—in its value, so silence, in any major work by Conrad, has exact but restless relations to what is being said. This restless shifting in the meanings of silences, as I indicated in the reading of "The End of The Tether" [in *Coercion to Speak*], was noticed by some of Conrad's earliest readers as an essential part of his ironic mastery and his involvement of the reader.

Thus we have broad historical and poetic uses of "silver" in this novel.

Silver is (1) a secondary currency, raising the issue of dependence; (2) the currency in the Americas which theoretically, if not in fact, might open the field of wealth out from the aristocracy and oligarchy toward the people; (3) an analogy to silence itself, not only as the "natural reserve" but because it is secondary and dependent. Silver is the only weapon of Sulaco against the outside world; silence is the only weapon of dependent persons who are being made to speak. By this technique of chiming or parallelism between the political economy and the dialogue economy of resistance, Conrad can give form to his precise insight that dialogue forms are not the "free" part of social life, *or* of the novel, but complex expressions of other working relations and currencies. And he does this not in an abstract way but by showing how each of the major characters makes a *distinctive* personal synthesis of the two Sulacan defenses, silver and silence, in the struggle to achieve some kind of autonomy. The limit of these varied attempts to achieve independence via dependent means is the desperate plural story of the different persons in the novel.

Conrad would later write about the structure of *A Personal Record*: "In the purposely mingled resonance of this double strain a friend here and there will perhaps detect a subtle accord." "Silver and silence" is another subtle accord, giving a strange new unity to a work. One of the major actions of *Nostromo*—if by action we mean with Francis Ferguson the way the poetic writing leads the mind of the reader to make conscious connections among previously segregated categories of experience—is the play between dependent dialogical manners and dependent monetary currency. Through this action *Nostromo* departs significantly from Conrad's earlier sense of dialogue as primarily a "physics" toward the sense that dialogue is primarily a "political economy" practiced by dependent persons. Though here too there is a great deal of attention to the physical force of noise, to physically amassed language, to dialogue as a meeting of weights, the more economic and historical action of "silver as silence" allows Conrad to offer a representation of the linguistic economies of colonized persons, in which they discover parallel ways of using money and silence together.

The central compounder of silence and silver is of course Charles Gould. He prizes silver as the key to Costaguana's redemption from restless politics; he maintains various aloof silences with Holroyd, with the local bureaucrats, and with Hirsch (who wants to sell him dynamite and hides, but has trouble getting him to talk at all). Gould takes part in such "degrading" marketplace dialogue as little as possible. His stolid "character" *is* this resistive alloy of silver and silence; but his imperial stance eventually extends to the dialogue of his marriage, which had been intimate, or at least tender, at first. "It was," we are told in a scene clarifying that the marriage is dead, "as if the inspiration of their early years had left her heart to turn into a wall of silver bricks, erected by the silent work of evil spirits, between her and her husband." There is no question that in the portrait of Charles Gould, taciturnity is a fetish as recurrent and as crucial as silver, or that Conrad does whatever he can to make us hear the near-silent chime, even at the risk of seeming grossly allegorical. As in *The Secret Agent*, there seems to be no way for political people to draw a line between the dialogue economy with which they meet the world and the dialogue of their marriages. To simplify somewhat, the reader is meant to reason in this way: in the context of this whole inquisitorial society, silence is the most common mode of defense, from the Indios to Monygham. Gould—hence his name—seems to personify the proverb, or cliché, that silence is golden, but the whole effect is vaguely ridiculous, and in reality, he is in possession of silence and silver, a more ambiguous, less absolute, more comically mechanical power.

That the Gould-silver irony is being emphasized throughout the novel to point to a general condition of dependency is clear enough within the novel itself, but can perhaps be reinforced by a look at Adam Mickiewicz. Here is Napoleon in *Pan Tadeusz*: "Such were the amusements and disputes of those days in the quiet Lithuanian village, where the rest of the world was swimming in tears and blood, and while that man, the god of war, surrounded by a cloud of regiments, armed with a thousand cannon, harnessing in his chariot golden eagles besides those of silver, was flying from the deserts of Libya to the lofty Alps, casting thunderbolt on thunderbolt, at the Pyramids, at Tabor, Matengo, Ulm, and Austerlitz. Victory and Conquest ran before and after him." For our purposes, the footnote to the same translation is useful when it informs us that "the reference is *of course* [my italics] to the golden eagles of Napoleon joined with the silver eagles of Poland." Of course? Probably not for most of Conrad's audience, but probably for Conrad himself. Here a little effort can help us become "familiar" with—that is, factitiously informed about—his non-English historical perspective. Charles Gould has, in relation to Sulaco, and then to Holroyd, a paradoxical *imperium in imperio*, an empire within an empire. During the Napoleonic era, the emblematic alliance between gold and silver gave brief hope that Poland might repel the Russian empire by a French alliance. There is no space here to survey nineteenth-century Franco-Polish relations, but only to note that by the 1890s, they had fallen somewhat into the shadow of a new French taste for things and novels Russian, which may be one reason why Conrad—unlike Mickiewicz and Juljusz Słowacki—chose England as his haven. The important point here is that gold and silver (Gould's silver mine) may be taken as an emblem of the unstable, unreliable, and often in the end disappointing alliance between a dependent nation and a great modernizing empire. Gould's silver alliance with the American golden boy Holroyd has *some* analogies to Poland's alliance with the golden power of Napoleon and its new world capitalism. It is not of course transparent symbolism—*Nostromo* is by no means "about" Poland's desire to secede from Russia—but the analogy helps us to feel Conrad's sense of "silver" as an ambiguous social force touched with dependency, weakness, and secondariness. The figure relies again on the reader's grasp of an uncertain "measure" and "disproportion" between two elements.

Silver has two nonmonetary meanings in the novel: it means "lesser" (like Poland) and it means "silence"; these together in turn mean the condition of dependency. To remain in Poland would have been to remain silent, or to have had to practice the arts of silent resistance. Mickiewicz, in the patriotic drama *Forefathers' Eve*, celebrates a Polish martyr who was messianically silent under interrogation but then was unable, after his release, to stop being silent with his friends and family. Conrad echoes this tragic fable when he shows how the necessary political silence invades and destroys the Gould marriage. But he was also skeptical of messianic or ineffable ideas of resistive silence in the first place. For him, silence, though sometimes admirable, is only *part* of the forced dialogue, not Romantically transcendent. The misreading of Conrad that takes taciturnity in his work as a sign of transcendence must be critically dispelled. Only the early sea stories have something of this character, and even there not without irony. We might almost go to the opposite extreme and say that a major theme in the novels from *Nostromo* to *Victory* is a near-systematic critique of his own and his reader's "taste for silence" to show that it is often dangerously impractical and sadly deceived. Gould's English taciturnity, his practical English version of Polish messianic silence, is one of numerous examples: a strong political reserve, praised and admired to a degree, but also exposed as personally destructive. It kills his marriage, and is perhaps also a partial delusion of independence in the political realm: "Charles Gould assumed that if the appearance of listening to deplorable balderdash must form part of the price he had to pay for being left unmolested, the obligation of uttering balderdash personally was by no means included in the bargain. He drew the line there." His gentlemanly rule in dialogue is not unlike Whalley's: he will suffer cant politely but not lower himself to actually speak it. But in the perpetual stream of critical irony the sentence that ends with the emphatic word *there* sounds like mockery of his arbitrary choice as one made from vanity, snobbism, and class safety, not from real dignity or truth. It is of extreme importance that with Holroyd, Gould does relent, does not draw the line. Even his silences with Holroyd have less dignity, and are more compromised, than those he practices with bureaucrats or merchants; they mean that he suppresses frankness to keep the backing. In all this, the silence and silver of Charles Gould add up to a "strong character" not nearly as autonomous or regal as it seems. Gould cannot make himself the Golfo Placido incarnate; his silences are human and dialogized, not natural and infinite, however successfully he seems to transcend.

Gould's character and consciousness are outlined in three ironically related meanings of the word *mine*: (1) the personal pronoun—possession as silent self-possession; (2) the quarry itself—possession as material wealth, with emphasis on ore as buried and secret; (3) the final threat to detonate the mine, turning it into a "mine" in the third sense, found particularly in the nautical lexicon: a hidden explosive sometimes set off by acoustic force. At least some of this forced polysemy is implied when Decoud scoffs bitterly: "He and his mine"; "he has his mine in his head." It is a negative progress of meanings which needs no paraphrase. The simplest, even most childish English word for the owning self is being redefined within the mode we are learning to recognize as forced dialogue. Ego is ultimately a property one can't refuse to have been given, and may be forced to define itself by a threat of self-destruction. This is why Charles Gould is not so much a great character as a great image of the tragic illusion in the idea that character is self-possession. "Mine" claims a self through an external object; this leads, logically, to the claim to the right to destroy the object. As in many places in Conrad's glossary, a word acquires its full meaning only when we perceive that identity has the unlikely structure of forced dialogue, involuntary relation. In addition, the polysemy of a word is not that of a "free" variety but of a dramatically conditioned forced relation. Gould's consciousness—the feeling throughout the novel that he embodies the ideas of "the mine," of strong secular identity as a logic of self-destructive pathos—implies that private identity paradoxically makes a last stand at the threat of self-destruction. Where Dickens ridicules the Coketown barons' threat to hurl their factories into the sea if the state intrudes, Gould's threat to detonate "his" mine, in a vast act of grotesque historical spite, though no less critically displayed as the logic of possessive identity, is no absurd bluff. And his attempt to make silence and silver the adequate sources of a locally strong personality is more than just stuffiness and archness. He expresses, through the logic of his class, one of the main themes of the novel—that the means, such as "property," by which dependent people must seek to establish independence are themselves dependent, and can become illusions of self-sufficiency, because all relation is in essence dependency, "destructive immersion." Only dependent instruments and compromising, coercive contracts are available.

The history of the Gould mine, called ironically a "Concession," and itself told as a forced dialogue, is one of the wittiest accounts of the origin of property in the English novel. "Concession" is a contractual speech act term used ironically here, since it was Gould Senior who conceded when he was forced by a political enemy to take on the mine as a tax burden, an unwanted, useless property. To own, for the Gould family, was originally to concede; property was not freedom but a forced relation. Later, Nostromo will become a more ambiguously forced owner of silver and silence in a similar concession of his best self to property. But the original outrage committed against Gould Senior, to *make him own* something, is very funny, with a sort of Balzacian acerbity about the idea that ownership is in essence free. The origin of this great family's wealth is a great crime against the family. English tradition usually associates ownership, like speech, with free choice. But here, to speak and to own are forced actions in which one must find a personality by choosing an answer from among limited options. This is how I would question, with more emphasis on circumstance and mutual force, Edward Said's thesis that Conrad's work in principle rejects "beginnings," and is concerned with tentative intentions rather than with origins. While this makes some sense in regard to Conrad's skepticism about authorship itself (though as already suggested he sometimes saw his writing as a forced contract), over and over, it seems to me, Conrad does present a clear notion of the forced origins of his various characters' lives in specific contracts they can't avoid. *Nostromo* as an action begins, comically, robustly, and primevally, when ownership of a useless mine is forced on Gould Senior; *The Secret Agent* begins when Verloc is forced, in dialogue with Vladimir, to produce terror; *Under Western Eyes* begins when Razumov is forced to talk with and shelter Haldin. Charles Gould's life, including his early study of mine engineering, is determined by the existence of the original Concession. He lives to reverse the status of the covenant that defeated his father, but though he then tries to forget the original involuntary character of the "mine" ownership, his life in fact has been defined by that coercion. Victory in forced dialogue is not the same as transcendence of its form.

This idea of ownership as forced possession, something inherited against one's will, like existence itself, both resembles and diverges from Harold Bloom's concept of poetic "influence." In *The Prelude* Wordsworth uses the term *inquisition* to describe his examination of himself for possible themes. As in Borges's reference to literature as "other inquisitions," the irony is infinite. Conrad, as his own work progressed, seems however to have turned, or to have tried to turn, partly away from the infinite ironic romance of self-inquisition (represented by the Romantically compelled speaker Marlow) toward the representation, during the period of the political novels, of limited, external, crude forced dialogues in the world. There is the hint of a suspicion that it might be a bad defense, a bad infinity, to always internalize the format of coercion to speak as poetic will. Poetics, in Bloomian Romanticism, may be the denial, by internalization, of the Oedipal order of forced dialogue in the outside world—the translation of inquisition into an inner feeling of compulsion to quarrel with a forebear or with oneself. In any case, Conrad turned from infinite self-inquisition to emphasize "objective" political scenes in which the enslaved, colonized, or dependent individual is made to speak, to own, to respond. In Bloom's signally moving personal terms, Gould's inheritance of the silver mine from his defeated father symbolizes Conrad's inheritance, from his own father and his "fathers," of Polish poetic dependency, Polish tragic "silence," Polish poetic minority in the greater world. And this is, to say the least, a viable reading. But Conrad's description of historical struggles for independence via dependent means is certainly also meant as a representation of actual political struggle by colonials against outside influences. This is one of the self-critical questions Conrad's later political novels direct, not always successfully, against his early work. He becomes convinced that the compulsion to speak does not always come from within, and that the political aspect of coercion to speak is at times disguised by inner agony.

Chronology

1857   Józef Teodor Konrad Korzeniowski born December 3, in Berdyczew, Poland, to Apollo Korzeniowski and Ewelina Bobrowska.

1862   Apollo Korzeniowski is exiled to Russia for his part in the Polish National Committee. His wife and son accompany him.

1865   Conrad's mother dies.

1869   Apollo Korzeniowski and son return to Cracow in February. Apollo dies on May 23.

1874   Conrad leaves Cracow for Marseilles, intending to become a sailor.

1875   Conrad is an apprentice aboard the *Mont Blanc*, bound for Martinique.

1877   Conrad is part owner of the *Tremolino*, which carries illegal arms to the Spanish pretender, Don Carlos.

1878   In February, after ending an unhappy love affair, Conrad attempts suicide by shooting himself. In June, he lands in England. He serves as ordinary seaman on the *Mavis*.

1883   Becomes mate on the ship *Riversdale*.

1884   Is second mate on the *Narcissus*, bound from Bombay to Dunkirk.

1886   Conrad becomes a naturalized British citizen.

1887   Is first mate on the *Highland Forest*.

1889   Begins writing *Almayer's Folly*.

1890   In May, Conrad leaves for the Congo as second in command of the S. S. *Roi de Belges*, later becoming commander.

1894   On January 14, he ends his sea career.

1895   Publishes *Almayer's Folly*. Writes *An Outcast of the Islands*. He is now living in London.

1896	Conrad marries Jessie George on March 24.
1897–1900	Writes *The Nigger of the "Narcissus," Heart of Darkness,* and *Lord Jim.*
1904	Completes *Nostromo.*
1905	Granted Civil List Pension. Travels in Europe for four months.
1907	Publishes *The Secret Agent.*
1911–12	Publishes *Under Western Eyes* and *'Twixt Land and Sea.*
1913	Publishes *Chance.*
1914	Writes *Victory.* Conrad visits Poland in July, where he is caught when the Great War breaks out on August 4. He escapes and returns safely to England in November.
1916	Conrad's son, Borys, is fighting on the French front.
1917	Publishes *The Shadow-Line* and prefaces to an edition of his collected works.
1918	Armistice, November 11.
1919	Conrad publishes *The Arrow of Gold.* He moves to Oswalds, Bishopsbourne, near Canterbury, where he spends his last years.
1920	Publishes *The Rescue.*
1924	In May, Conrad declines a knighthood. After an illness, he dies of a heart attack on August 3. He is buried in Canterbury.
1925	The incomplete *Suspense* published. *Tales of Hearsay* published.
1926	*Last Essays* published.

Contributors

HAROLD BLOOM, Sterling Professor of the Humanities at Yale University, is the author of *The Anxiety of Influence, Poetry and Repression*, and many other volumes of literary criticism. His forthcoming study, *Freud: Transference and Authority*, attempts a full-scale reading of all of Freud's major writings. A MacArthur Prize Fellow, he is general editor of five series of literary criticism published by Chelsea House.

ROBERT PENN WARREN is our most distinguished living man-of-letters. His best-known novels are *All the King's Men* and *World Enough and Time*. His other crucial books include *Selected Poems* and *Selected Essays*.

DOROTHY VAN GHENT taught at Kansas University and the University of Vermont. Her numerous publications include *The English Novel: Form and Function* and *Keats: The Myth of the Hero*.

GEORGE LEVINE is Professor of English at Rutgers University. He is the author of *The Boundaries of Fiction* and *The Realistic Imagination: English Fiction from Frankenstein to Lady Chatterly*.

KIERNAN RYAN is College Lecturer in English at New Hall, Cambridge.

T. McALINDON is Senior Lecturer in English at Hull University, England. He is the author of *Shakespeare and Decorum*.

MARTIN PRICE is Sterling Professor of English at Yale University. His previous books include *Swift's Rhetorical Art: A Study in Structure and Meaning, To the Palace of Wisdom: Studies in Order and Energy from Dryden to Blake*, and a number of edited volumes on literature of the seventeenth, eighteenth, and nineteenth centuries.

STEPHEN K. LAND is the author of *From Signs to Propositions: The Concept of Form in Eighteenth-Century Semantic Theory, Kett's Rebellion: The Norfolk Rising of 1549*, and *Conrad and the Paradox of Plot*.

AARON FOGEL is Assistant Professor of English at Boston University. He is the author of *Coercion to Speak: Conrad's Poetics of Dialogue*.

Bibliography

Baines, Jocelyn. *Joseph Conrad: A Critical Biography*. New York: McGraw-Hill, 1960.

Beach, Joseph Warren. "Impressionism: Conrad." In *The Twentieth-Century Novel: Studies in Technique*, 337–65. New York: Appleton-Century, 1932.

Berman, Jeffrey. *Joseph Conrad: Writing as Rescue*. New York: Astra Books, 1977.

Bradbrook, M. C. *Joseph Conrad: Poland's English Genius*. Cambridge: Cambridge University Press, 1941.

Brown, Robert. "Integrity and Self-Deception." *The Critical Review* 25 (1983): 115–31.

Bufkin, Ernest C. "Conrad, Grand Opera, and *Nostromo*." *Nineteenth-Century Fiction* 30 (1975): 206–14.

Carpenter, Richard C. "The Geography of Costaguana, or Where Is Sulaco?" *Journal of Modern Literature* 5 (1976): 321–26.

Chapple, J. A. V. "Conrad." In *The English Novel*. Select Bibliographical Guides, edited by A. E. Dyson. London: Oxford University Press, 1974.

Conradiana: A Journal of Joseph Conrad Studies, 1968–.

Conroy, Mark. "Lost in Azuera: The Fate of Sulaco and Conrad's *Nostromo*." *Glyph* 8 (1981): 148–69.

Cox, Roger L. "Conrad's *Nostromo* as Boatswain." *MLN* 74 (1959): 303–6.

Curle, Richard. *The Last Twelve Years of Joseph Conrad*. Garden City, N.Y.: Doubleday, 1928.

Daleski, H. M. *Joseph Conrad: The Way of Dispossession*. London: Faber & Faber, 1977.

Ehrsam, T. G. *A Bibliography of Joseph Conrad*. Metuchen, N.J.: Scarecrow Press, 1969.

Ellmann, Richard, and Charles Feidelson, eds. *The Modern Tradition*. New York: Oxford University Press, 1965.

Fogel, Aaron. *Coercion to Speak: Conrad's Poetics of Dialogue*. Cambridge: Harvard University Press, 1985.

Ford, Ford Madox. *Joseph Conrad: A Personal Remembrance*. Boston: Little, Brown, 1924.

Galsworthy, John. "Reminiscences of Conrad." In *Castles in Spain and Other Screeds*, 99–126. New York: Scribner's, 1927.

Garnett, Edward. *Letters from Joseph Conrad, 1895–1924*. Indianapolis: Bobbs-Merrill, 1928.

Gekoski, R. A. *Conrad: The Moral World of the Novelist*. New York: Harper & Row, 1978.

Gillon, Adam. *The Eternal Solitary*. New York: Bookman Associates, 1960.

———. *Joseph Conrad*. Boston: Twayne, 1982.

Gillon, Adam, and Ludwik Krzyzanowski, eds. *Joseph Conrad: Commemorative Essays*. New York: Astra Books, 1975.

Guerard, Albert J. *Conrad the Novelist*. Cambridge: Harvard University Press, 1958.

————. *Joseph Conrad*. New York: New Directions, 1947.

Hay, Eloise Knapp. "Joseph Conrad and Impressionism." *Journal of Aesthetics and Art Criticism* 34 (1975): 137–44.

————. *The Political Novels of Joseph Conrad*. Chicago: University of Chicago Press, 1963.

James, Henry. *Notes on Novelists*. New York: Scribner's, 1914.

Jean-Aubry, Gérard. *Joseph Conrad: Life and Letters*. London: Heinemann, 1927.

————. *The Sea Dreamer: A Definitive Biography of Joseph Conrad*. Translated by Helen Sebba. Garden City, N.Y.: Doubleday, 1957.

Jenkins, Gareth. "Conrad's *Nostromo* and History." *Literature and History* 6 (1977): 138–78.

Johnson, Bruce M. *Conrad's Models of Mind*. Minneapolis: University of Minnesota Press, 1971.

Joseph Conrad Today: The Newsletter of the Joseph Conrad Society of America, 1975–.

Karl, Frederick R. *Joseph Conrad: The Three Lives*. New York: Farrar, Straus & Giroux, 1979.

————. *A Reader's Guide to Joseph Conrad*, rev. ed. New York: Noonday Press, 1969.

Kermode, Frank. "Secrets and Narrative Sequence." *Critical Inquiry* 7 (1980): 83–101.

Kotzin, Michael C. "A Fairy-Tale Pattern in Conrad's *Nostromo*." *Modern British Literature* 2 (1977): 200–214.

La Bossière, Camille R. *Joseph Conrad and the Science of Unknowing*. Fredericton, N.B., Canada: York Press, 1979.

Leavis, F. R. *The Great Tradition*. London: Chatto & Windus, 1948.

————. "Joseph Conrad." *The Sewanee Review* 46 (1958): 179–200.

McLauchlin, Juliet. *Conrad: Nostromo*. London: Edward Arnold, 1969.

Meyer, Bernard C. *Joseph Conrad: A Psychoanalytic Biography*. Princeton: Princeton University Press, 1967.

Miller, J. Hillis. *Poets of Reality: Six Twentieth-Century Writers*. Cambridge: Harvard University Press, 1965.

Moser, Thomas. *Joseph Conrad: Achievement and Decline*. Hamden, Conn.: Archon, 1957.

Mudrick, Marvin, ed. *Conrad: A Collection of Critical Essays*. Englewood Cliffs, N.J.: Prentice-Hall, 1966.

Nettels, Elsa. *James and Conrad*. Athens: University of Georgia Press, 1977.

Oates, Joyce Carol. "'The Immense Indifference of Things': The Tragedy of Conrad's *Nostromo*." *Novel: A Forum on Fiction* 9, no. 1 (Fall 1975): 5–22.

Palmer, John A. *Joseph Conrad's Fiction: A Study in Literary Growth*. Ithaca, N.Y.: Cornell University Press, 1968.

Ray, Martin. "Conrad and Decoud." *Polish Review* 29, no. 3 (1984): 53–64.

Schwarz, Daniel R. "Conrad's Quarrel with Politics: The Disputed Family in *Nostromo*." *University of Toronto Quarterly* 47 (1977): 37–55.

Sherry, Norman. *Conrad's Eastern World*. Cambridge: Cambridge University Press, 1966.

————, ed. *Conrad: The Critical Heritage*. London: Routledge & Kegan Paul, 1973.

————, ed. *Joseph Conrad: A Commemoration*. New York: Harper & Row, 1977.

Stallman, Robert W., ed. *The Art of Joseph Conrad: A Critical Symposium*. East Lansing: Michigan State University Press, 1960.

Tennant, Roger. *Joseph Conrad: A Biography*. New York: Atheneum, 1981.

Thornburn, David. *Conrad's Romanticism*. New Haven: Yale University Press, 1974.

Verluen, Jan. *The Stone Horse: A Study of the Function of the Minor Characters in Conrad's Nostromo*. Groningen, The Netherlands: Bouma's Boekhuis, 1978.

Whitehead, Lee M. "Recent Conrad Criticism." *Dalhousie Review* 61, no. 4 (1981–82): 743–49.

Wiley, Paul L. *Conrad's Measure of Man*. Madison: University of Wisconsin Press, 1954.

Yelton, D. C. *Mimesis and Metaphor: An Inquiry into the Genesis and Scope of Conrad's Symbolic Imagery*. The Hague: Mouton, 1967.

Young, Vernon. "Joseph Conrad: Outline for a Reconsideration." *The Hudson Review* 2 (1949): 5–19.

Zabel, Morton Dauwen. *Craft and Character in Modern Fiction*. New York: Viking, 1957.

————, ed. Introduction to *The Portable Conrad*, 1–47. New York: Viking, 1947.

Acknowledgments

" 'The Great Mirage': Conrad and *Nostromo*" by Robert Penn Warren from *Selected Essays* by Robert Penn Warren, © 1951 by Random House, Inc. Reprinted by permission of the author and Random House.

"Guardianship of the Treasure: *Nostromo*" (originally entitled "*Nostromo*") by Dorothy Van Ghent from *Joseph Conrad: A Collection of Criticism*, edited by Frederick R. Karl, © 1975 by McGraw-Hill, Inc. This essay originally appeared as the "Introduction" to *Nostromo*, © 1961 by Holt, Rinehart & Winston, Inc. Reprinted by permission of Holt, Rinehart & Winston, Inc.

"Continuities and Discontinuities: *Middlemarch* and *Nostromo*" (originally entitled "The Hero as Dilettante: *Middlemarch* and *Nostromo*") by George Levine from *The Realistic Imagination: English Fiction from Frankenstein to Lady Chatterley* by George Levine, © 1981 by the University of Chicago. Reprinted by permission of the University of Chicago Press.

"Revelation and Repression in Conrad's *Nostromo*" by Kiernan Ryan from *The Uses of Fiction: Essays on the Modern Novel in Honor of Arnold Kettle*, edited by Douglas Jefferson and Graham Martin, © 1982 by the Open University Press. Reprinted by permission.

"*Nostromo*: Conrad's Organicist Philosophy of History" by T. McAlindon from *Mosaic: A Journal for the Interdisciplinary Study of Literature* 15, no. 3 (September 1982), © 1982 by Mosaic. Reprinted by permission.

"The Limits of Irony" (originally entitled "Conrad: The Limits of Irony") by Martin Price from *Forms of Life: Character and Moral Imagination in the Novel* by Martin Price, © 1983 by Yale University. Reprinted by permission of Yale University Press.

"Four Views of the Hero" (originally entitled "*Nostromo*") by Stephen K. Land from *Conrad and the Paradox of Plot* by Stephen K. Land, © 1984 by Stephen K. Land. Reprinted by permission of Macmillan Publishers Ltd.

"Silver and Silence: Dependent Currencies in *Nostromo*" by Aaron Fogel from *Coercion to Speak: Conrad's Poetics of Dialogue* by Aaron Fogel, © 1985 by the President and Fellows of Harvard College. Reprinted by permission of Harvard University Press.

Index

Absalom! Absalom! (Faulkner), 110
Almayer's Folly, 81, 107
Ambassadors, The (James), 3
As I Lay Dying (Faulkner), 3
"Autocracy and War," 21
Avellanos, Antonia (*Nostromo*), 14, 83–84
Avellanos, Don José (*Nostromo*): characteristics of, 13, 53, 71, 113–14; Decoud compared to, 85; as historical figure, 14, 50

Bakhtin, Mikhail, 106, 118
Barrios, General, 37
Bartleby the Scrivener (Melville), 112
Bento, Guzman, 65
Berón, Father, 65
Bleak House (Dickens), 105
Bloom, Harold, 124, 125
"Books," 18–19, 20
Borges, Jorge Luis, 125
Braudel, Fernand, 105
Bryan, William Jennings, 119
Burnaby, Frederick, 57
"Burnt Norton" (T. S. Eliot), 68

Cantos, The (Pound), 107
Carlyle, Thomas, 2, 57–58, 60, 62, 65, 67–68
Chance, 8, 20–21
Commedia, La (Dante), 36
Conn-Eda, 26–27, 31
Conquest of Mexico, The (Prescott), 60
Conquest of Peru, The (Prescott), 60
Conrad, Joseph: as artist, 20; illness of, 8–9; letters of, 112; literary influences on, 2, 52, 57–58, 60–61, 62, 67–68, 106, 107, 112, 116; as philo-sophical novelist, 21; Polish background of, 104, 118, 121; political conservatism of, 45–46; skepticism of, 9–10, 20
Conrad's fiction: alienation as theme in, 8; fables in, 7, 19–20; fidelity as theme in, 7, 8, 10; human solidarity as theme in, 7–8, 10, 11, 18; humor in, 111, 112–13; idealization in, 10–11, 12; illusion as theme in, 11–12, 14; job sense as theme in, 7, 8; names in, 60; redemption as theme in, 8, 9, 14; "seeing" in, 2, 20, 21, 39, 44, 45; skepticism in, 9, 11, 12–14; "true lie" as motif in, 12. *See also specific works*
Corbelán, Father (*Nostromo*), 37, 53, 64–65
Crankshaw, Edward, 20
Criticism and Ideology (Eagleton), 54

Daleski, H. M., 76
Dante Alighieri, 36
Decoud, Don Martin (*Nostromo*), 5–6, 83–86; Avellanos compared to, 85; historical and political beliefs of, 58–59, 66, 84–87; idealism of, 73; irony in character of, 73–75; letter to sister of, 15, 34; name, significance of, 116; ordeal of, 31–32; as outsider, 83; rationalism of, 32; Sebastian Van Storck compared to, 2; silver, meaning of, for, 24–25; skepticism of, 12–13, 74, 83, 84, 86–87; solitude of, 3, 6, 8, 78, 86–87; suicide of, 3, 5, 6, 25, 32, 54, 66–67, 78, 86–87
Dickens, Charles, 7, 73, 105, 109, 118, 123
Dostoyevski, Fyodor, 106, 118

Eagleton, Terry, 54
Eliot, George, 40
Eliot, T. S., 68
End of the Tether, The, 101, 107

Faulkner, William, 3, 110
Ferguson, Francis, 120
Fitzgerald, F. Scott, 3
Flaubert, Gustave, 2, 52, 112, 119
Fleishman, Avrom, 104
Forefathers' Eve (Mickiewicz), 122

Galsworthy, John, 9, 10, 14
Garnett, Edward, 21
Gide, André, 55
Golden Bowl, The (James), 3
Gould, Charles (*Nostromo*), 13, 81; as aris-
tocrat, 93; atonement of, 30; William
Jennings Bryan compared to, 119;
Nicholas Bulstrode compared to, 41;
Hirsch, relationship with, 120;
Holroyd, relationship with, 120, 123;
idealism of, 74–75, 93; irony in character of, 15, 77; as king, 25, 50, 61–
62, 63; marriage of, 24, 25, 30, 50,
121, 122; materialism of, 15, 65, 82–
83; mine, meaning of for, 123–24,
125; ordeal of, 29–31; as outsider, 83;
in palazzo scene, 69–70; as realist,
29, 71, 72; silence of, 120–21, 122–23;
silver, meaning of for, 24, 63, 120–21,
122–23; as "stranger knight," 25
Gould, Emilia (*Nostromo*): barrenness of,
24, 25, 30; as fairy princess, 25, 30;
idealism of, 70, 71; irony in character
of, 77; lifelessness of, 53; marriage of,
24, 25, 30, 50, 121, 122; Monygham,
relationship with, 31, 88; in palazzo
scene, 69–70; as queen, 61–62; as
saint, 65; silver, meaning of for, 24
Graham, R. B. Cunninghame, 9, 106, 107,
116, 117
Graver, Lawrence, 105, 106
Great Gatsby, The (Fitzgerald), 3
Guerard, Albert, Jr., 13, 15

"Hadji Murad" (Tolstoy), 4, 6
Hardy, Thomas, 10, 14
Hay, Eloise Knapp, 109

Heart of Darkness, 3, 58; capitalism in, 17;
character patterning in, 101; colonialism in, 46; illusion as theme in,
12; imperialism in, 14, 17, 47; Kurtz's
role in, 8, 10, 46–47, 100, 101, 119;
Marlow's role in, 7, 10, 46–47, 119;
parallelism in, 119; "true lie" as
motif in, 12
Hemingway, Ernest, 3
Heracleitus, 5
Hirsch, Señor (*Nostromo*), 36–37, 90, 120
Holroyd (*Nostromo*), 29, 71; filibustering
of, 107, 108; Gould, Charles, relationship with, 120, 123
Housman, A. E., 10

Imaginary Portraits (Pater), 2
Intention and Method (Said), 44
Introduction to the English Novel, An
(Kettle), 43

James, Henry, 2, 3, 42
Joyce, James, 68

Kettle, Arnold, 43, 51

Leavis, F. R., 13, 21, 54, 103, 113
Lewes, George Henry, 39
Little Dorrit (Dickens), 70
Lord Jim, 3, 58, 71; Brown's role in, 10;
Jim's role in, 8, 77, 89–90; Marlow's
role in, 77; Stein's role in, 11
Lukács, Georg, 52

McFee, William, 8
Marius the Epicurean (Pater), 2
Maupassant, Guy de, 2
Melville, Herman, 112
Mickiewicz, Adam, 121, 122
Middlemarch (George Eliot), 40–42
Miller, J. Hillis, 44
Mitchell, Captain Joseph (*Nostromo*), 15–
16, 33–34, 48, 49, 76, 113
Moby-Dick (Melville), 104
Mogreb-el-Acksa (Graham), 106, 107, 116
Montero, Pedrito (*Nostromo*), 14, 36, 53
Monygham, Doctor (*Nostromo*), 87–92;

characteristics of, 72, 87, 88, 113; Emilia Gould, relationship with, 31, 72, 88; Jim compared to, 71, 89–90; ordeal of, 31; as outsider, 83, 88; persecution of, 87–88; redemption of, 8

"Narrate or Describe?" (Lukács), 52
Natural Supernaturalism, 2
Nigger of the "Narcissus," The: character patterning in, 101; preface to, 2, 9, 39, 44, 45; Wait's role in, 100, 101
Nostromo (Fidanza, Captain Giovanni Battista) (Nostromo): clothing of, 98–99; Columbus compared to, 62; competence of, 65–66; death of, 3, 6, 17, 28, 66; fidelity of, 28; as indispensable man, 29, 75; irony in character of, 5, 75, 100; lifelessness of, 53; as man of the people and natural man, 4, 27–28, 29, 35, 37, 93; names of, 65–66, 96, 117; as outsider, 83; as peripheral character, 49–50; Razumov and Verloc compared to, 92, 93, 101; reputation of, 75, 95–96; as saint, 65, 66; silence of, 124; silver, meaning of for, 75–76, 96–97, 100, 124; uniqueness of character of, 3–4; Violas, relationship with, 94–95
Nostromo: atonement as theme in, 30; bureaucracy in, 76; capitalism in, 14, 15, 17, 47; colonialism in, 63–64, 115, 118, 125; Conn-Eda compared to, 26–27, 31; Conrad's opinion of, 54–55; demonism in, 36; descriptive style of, 51–52, 53, 62–63, 113–14; dialogical method of, 113–14, 115, 119; fable, folklore, and mythical elements in, 19, 23–33, 36–37, 115; filibuster as method in, 107–10, 114; "freebooting" in, 107–9; geography in, 19, 32–33, 36, 105, 107, 115; Heart of Darkness compared to, 119; heteroglossia in, 118; as historical novel, 14, 41–42, 48, 51–52, 53–54, 58–60, 68, 118; how to read, 34; humor in, 37, 111, 117, 124; idealization in, 14; illusion as theme in, 14, 70, 71, 73, 74, 78–79; imperialism in, 14, 15, 17, 76; irony in, 66–67, 69–79, 98; Middlemarch compared to, 40–42; mine as symbol in, 24, 123; Mogreb-el-Acksa compared to, 116–17; names in, 65–66, 96, 116–18; palazzo scene in, 69–70; parallelism in, 119; parrot in, 70, 110–11, 112; political aspect of, 14, 17, 50, 86, 87, 104–5, 106, 115, 122, 125; polyglossia in, 116, 118; reader's and writer's role in, 6, 52–53, 118; religion in, 62–66; repression and revelation in, 45–46, 47–51, 53–55; scale of, 103–7, 114; "seeing" in, 34–35; silence as theme in, 114–16, 119–21, 124; silver as symbol in, 23–25, 37, 114–15, 118–21, 122, 124; treasure as theme in, 23, 30, 33, 36, 37; unpopularity of, 110. See also specific characters

Othello (Shakespeare), 3
Outcast of the Islands, An, 81, 86, 100, 101

Pan Tadeusz (Mickiewicz), 121
Pater, Walter, 2, 39–40
Pelopponesian Wars, The (Thucydides), 107
Personal Record, A, 7, 8, 21, 120
Pickwick Papers, The (Dickens), 109
Pound, Ezra, 107
Prelude, The (Wordsworth), 124–25
Prescott, W. H., 60–61, 62

Rabelais, François, 106
Reign of Ferdinand and Isabella, The (Prescott), 60, 61
Ride to Khiva (Burnaby), 57
"Rime of the Ancient Mariner, The" (Coleridge), 32
Rover, The, 68, 107
Ruskin, John, 2

Said, Edward, 40, 41, 42, 44, 104
Sartor Resartus (Carlyle), 57–58
Secret Agent, The, 3, 70, 78, 103–4; as political novel, 17, 106, 121; Verloc's role in, 92, 93, 97, 101, 102, 124
Shadow-Line, The, 7
Shakespeare, William, 7
Sienkiewicz, Henryk, 104
Slowacki, Juljusz, 122

Spoils of Poynton, The (James), 2
Stevenson, Robert Louis, 10
Sun Also Rises, The (Hemingway), 3
Suspense, 68
Swift, Jonathan, 106, 107, 110

Tale of a Tub, A (Swift), 110
Tennyson, Alfred, 10
Thucydides, 107
Titanic essays, 119
Tolstoy, Leo, 4, 106
Turgenev, Ivan, 106
"Two Songs from a Play" (Yeats), 19
Typhoon, 8

Uccello, Paolo, 36
Under Western Eyes, 3, 78; Haldin's role in, 10, 97, 124; human solidarity as theme in, 16–17; as political novel, 17, 106; Razumov's role in, 8, 18, 92, 93, 101, 102, 124; "true lie" as motif in, 12

Victory, 3, 8, 10, 92
Viola, Giorgio (*Nostromo*): descriptions of, 53, 63, 113; as historical figure, 14, 35, 50, 93–94, 100; idealism of, 93–94, 100–101
Viola, Giselle (*Nostromo*), 99–100
Viola, Linda (*Nostromo*), 99–100
Viola, Teresa (*Nostromo*), 93–95, 97–98, 116

War and Peace (Tolstoy), 40, 104
Watt, Ian, 2
"Well Done," 7
What Maisie Knew (James), 2
Wordsworth, William, 124–25

Yeats, William Butler, 19, 68
"Youth," 1–2, 40, 57, 58

Zabel, Morton, 8
Zola, Émile, 52